"Does Wednesday Mean Mom's House or Dad's?"

"Does Wednesday Mean Mom's House or Dad's?"

Parenting Together While Living Apart

MARC J. ACKERMAN

John Wiley & Sons, Inc.

New York • Chichester • Brisbane • Toronto • Singapore • Weinheim

This text is printed on acid-free paper.

Copyright © 1997 by Marc J. Ackerman
Published by John Wiley & Sons, Inc.

All rights reserved. Published simultaneously in Canada.

Though this book is nonfiction, the names and distinguishing traits of all clients and individuals mentioned in the book have been changed.

Reproduction or translation of any part of this work beyond that permitted by Section 107 or 108 of the 1976 United States Copyright Act without the permission of the copyright owner is unlawful. Requests for permission or further information should be addressed to the Permissions Department, John Wiley & Sons, Inc., 605 Third Avenue, New York, NY 10158-0012

This publication is designed to provide accurate and authoritative information in regard to the subject matter covered. It is sold with the understanding that the publisher is not engaged in rendering professional services. If legal, accounting, medical, psychological, or any other expert assistance is required, the services of a competent professional person should be sought.

Library of Congress Cataloging-in-Publication Data

Ackerman, Marc J.
    "Does Wednesday mean mom's house or dad's?" : parenting together
while living apart / by Marc J. Ackerman.
        p.   cm.
    Includes bibliographical references.
    ISBN 0-471-13048-6 (pbk. : alk. paper)
    1. Parenting, Part-time—United States.   2. Divorce—United
States—Psychological aspects.   3. Children of divorced parents—
United States.   4. Children of divorced parents—United States—
Psychology.   I. Title.
HQ755.8.A25   1996
649'.1—dc20   96-18380

Printed in the United States of America

10 9 8 7 6 5 4 3 2

This Book is Dedicated to:

Aaron, Adam, Alexandra, Amy, Andrea, Angela, Anthony, Brandon, Brian, Caitlin, Cameron, Casey, Christian, Christina, Christine, Christopher, Chuck, Daniel, David, Elizabeth, Eric, Evan, Grant, Jamie, Janine, Jason, Jennifer, Jonathan, Jordan, Joseph, Julia, Katherine, Kelly, Kenneth, Kevin, Lawrence, Lindsey, Marcy, Mary, Maureen, Megan, Melissa, Michael, Patrick, Raymond, Robert, Ryan, Scott, Shannon, Stacy, Todd, Vincent, William . . .

This book is dedicated to the above-named children and to all other children who have been forced to endure their parents fighting for years about custody-related issues. To those, and all others, whose parents believe that winning is more important than the well-being of their children, I hope you overcome these obstacles, and best wishes to you.

Preface

Divorce is one of the most difficult transitions you will ever make in your life. It is a dramatic, time-consuming, frustrating, stressful process that leaves many adults reeling from the extreme changes it creates in their lives. Swings in financial and social status, emotional upheaval, and grief over failed expectations and the loss of the marriage partner have a tremendous effect on lives.

As difficult as divorce is for adults, it has the potential to be absolutely devastating for children. Divorce impacts all children, regardless of age. It shatters their underlying security and throws them into a state of limbo because from one day to the next they don't know what to expect from life or from their parents. They feel as if they can count on nothing and no one.

Depending on their age, children experience guilt, believing the divorce is their fault, anger, sometimes bordering on outright rage, sadness, confusion, and a sense of helplessness that makes them anxious, forlorn, and frightened. They even have bouts of feeling abandoned and rejected, especially when one of you moves out of the home. Divorce adversely affects their schoolwork, method of play, and even their health.

As the divorce and custody processes unfold (they are inseparable if you have children), children's emotions and reactions to their situations change. These swings generally dissipate as some of their fears are alleviated. For example, a child often feels abandoned because Mom or Dad has moved out, but if, over the course of the next few weeks or months, that child sees that you are still around through planned visits and that you can still help with homework, play basketball, and so on, the feelings of abandonment and rejection normally disappear.

The extent to which your child is affected by divorce depends largely on you. You are the operative figure in this picture, but you are not the most important person to be considered in it, even though you and/or your spouse are responsible for triggering the process. If you have children, they are the single most important consideration in the divorce and custody processes.

Most separations or divorces occur when children are under the age of 12 and are still concrete thinkers, meaning they don't understand all the subtleties and underlying influences on such abstract concepts as falling in and out of love. Many occurrences must be explained to them, even ones that as an adult you may not see the need to explain. Children can be made more comfortable at each stage of the divorce and custody processes if you tell them specifically what you expect to happen and how it will happen.

How and what you tell them and under what circumstances you tell them is critical to the way children react to the news of your separation and accept or reject it. For example, it is okay for children to know that the separation is taking place because you and the other parent don't love each other anymore. However, it is not necessary, but instead destructive, to go through small details about affairs or other problems.

It is important for you to consistently assure your children that although you and your spouse have fallen out of love, you have not fallen out of love with them. Explain to them that the love bond between children and their parents occurs at birth and that it will last throughout their lives, that you will not unlearn to love them.

Knowledge is one of the keys to lessening the impact of divorce on children. You must learn from the outset of your divorce how to handle children. You must know how to inform and approach them to lessen their emotional load and how to help them deal with rapid changes in their lives as those changes occur and whenever possible, in advance of their occurrence.

This book is designed to guide you through the divorce and custody processes with the best interests of your children as your primary concern. You will discover that it takes a good deal of focus, self-control, and selflessness to keep children in that number one priority space. You will also find that if you and your spouse can exercise enough self-discipline to contain your anger toward each other and work things out based on what is best for your children, you will also benefit.

As you read on, you will find information that will help you break the news of divorce to your children, keep them informed without overburdening them, and enable you to anticipate behavioral and emotional responses at various ages of your children and at various stages of the divorce and custody processes. This book will even help you simplify their lives and yours through the use of highly adaptable schedules and plans for visitation.

As you move through your divorce, and find yourself repeatedly tested and stretched to and beyond your limits, if you have any doubts about keeping your children as your first priority, just look at their faces and really hear what they are saying when they ask you where they are going to live, with whom, and for how long. In my practice, I have dealt with more than a thousand children who were in the midst of custody and placement battles. One need only look at and listen to them to understand what divorce does to them and to realize that winning is never more important than the well-being of your children. This message is repeated throughout these pages. Keep it in mind as you help your children figure out if Wednesday means Mom's house or Dad's.

M.A.

Acknowledgments

In August 1994, I was sitting in my office, engaged in a therapy session with a couple who was in the process of divorcing. They suggested to me that since I had already written a book for psychologists and another book for attorneys, I should write a book for parents who were in the throes of divorce. Liking the idea, I immediately contacted Kelly Franklin, my editor at John Wiley & Sons, Inc. She encouraged me to write the book, but also informed me that it would be the most difficult book that I had ever written. I scoffed at this suggestion. Having authored or coauthored dozens of research works or books, I knew that this would be among the easiest of tasks I had performed. I was wrong and Kelly was right. A tremendous debt of gratitude is owed to Kelly for sticking with this project, encouraging me to continue even though I felt at times like I would never reach the level of satisfaction required, and for providing thoughtful editing and commentary. Perhaps her most important role was putting me in touch with Toni Reinhold. Kelly suggested that Toni was needed to convert this book from a dry text with important content to one that was easily readable. Toni, through her words, breathed life into the concepts that I was trying to present, without changing the content of the material. I doubt that this project would have reached the point of publication without Toni's diligence, perseverance, and thoughtful, encouraging commentary. A deep sincere thanks to both Kelly and Toni.

A number of attorneys helped in preparing this manuscript by providing suggestions, material, or editing. They include: Lee Calvey, Martin Gagne, Susan Hansen, James Podell, Peggy Podell, Nina Vitek. A special thanks goes to attorney Peggy Podell, who provided numerous suggestions for the section on choosing an attorney, and to attorney Nina Vitek, who provided invaluable material about international laws regarding custody matters.

As is true of all the books I have written, deep appreciation and thanks go to my wife, Stephanie Ackerman, and office manager, Lynn Spencer. As in the past, Stephanie provided valuable editing. Her honest criticisms, although somewhat harsh at times, were what the book needed to reach the level of excellence that was desired. Lynn, as always, typed the manuscript, made the revisions, dealt with me pacing around the office trying to meet deadlines, and did it all without complaining.

Contents

Contents

▼
Chapter

1

A House Divided

The end of your marriage is in sight, but you still live with the hope that somehow, some way, you'll be able to resolve the problems and differences that are wrenching you and your spouse apart. You deny that your difficulties are insurmountable or could be so overpowering that they would nullify the investment of time, energy, emotions, and money you've made in your spouse and the two of you as a couple. You wonder what else you might do to make your marriage better and restore the love that brought you together in the first place.

You think about your children, recognizing that (in all probability) they love both of you and would be better off in a whole family instead of a broken one. You are torn by indecision and guilt, born of questions about whether it is better to stay in a marriage void of happiness and fulfillment for the sake of your children.

Before you have a chance to resolve these issues, you open the mail or answer the door or have a discussion with your spouse and discover that what you've been dreading has now become your reality—YOU ARE GETTING DIVORCED. For a moment, the world seems to stop on its axis. What will you do? What about the children? How will you survive? Where will you go? What will people say? You wonder if life is over and if things will ever be the same.

Although your life and the lives of your children and your spouse will never be the same, life does not end with divorce. You will survive. Sometimes it is in everybody's best interest to live apart, but if children are involved, your household must continue standing, albeit under different roofs. You face a long and probably difficult road along which many decisions will have to be made, including determining custody and placement for your children, visitation times, discipline issues, financial arrangements, and schooling.

Throughout the divorce process, you will become involved in counseling, mediation, and court hearings. You will also need professional advice from lawyers, psychologists, social workers, and judges. You will be called on to be strong when you feel weak, to advance when you are tired, and to repeatedly put your children's interests before your own. The focus of this book is the well-being of your children. This is one of the facts about divorce—children must come first.

Facts about Divorce

If you are going to negotiate a divorce with your children's best interests as your focal point, you must be aware of some other important facts about divorce.

Fact 1: Divorce is always painful for children, no matter how old they are.

You cannot change that, but as parents, YOU will determine the degree of heartache some children will experience. In my practice, I speak with many divorcing parents who are concerned about how their divorce will affect their children and want to protect them from its negative impact. Sadly, I have to tell them that they cannot protect their children from the pain and grief of divorce, but they can keep the hurt and damage at a minimum through their own behavior. The more fighting, hatred, and lack of cooperation that exists, the harder it will be on the children.

Fact 2: Divorce does not end the relationship between spouses, it just changes the rules of the relationship.

Many people get divorced with the notion, "I'm going to finally get rid of this guy" or "I'm not going to have to listen to her anymore." The fact is that if you have children under the age of 18, you will be required to have some sort of relationship with your ex-spouse until your child reaches 18.

Although your relationship will continue on some level, children must learn that life will never be the same after the divorce. It is not uncommon for children to fantasize that someday life will return to the way it was prior to the divorce. This is not possible and the sooner everyone understands that, the easier life will be. If your children have difficulty grasping this, it may be necessary to get outside help, such as counseling.

It's important at this time to give your children as much stability as possible. Direct your energy toward helping them adjust to this new life.

Fact 3: You are not the only parent going through divorce.

Parents become very self-focused during the divorce process. They often feel they are the only ones having to change their daily routine, work schedule, and time with the children. Your former partner is going through the same changes. Recognize that every change you must make, he or she must also make. In addition, the moving parent will have to make significantly more changes than the parent who remains at home, and may actually be going through more adjustments.

3

Fact 4: You do not have to hate your spouse to get divorced.

It's not unusual for a parent midway through the divorce process to question whether the divorce should even take place. The assumption that people often make is that if they are getting divorced, they should hate their spouse. Extending that logic, if they don't, they question whether they should be getting divorced at all.

There are things you are apt to still like about your partner even if you are getting divorced, and those ambivalent feelings can lead to confusion about the impending separation. If the things you don't like about your partner outweigh the things you do like, the decision to divorce is probably a sound one. However, when the things you disliked have changed, then questioning the divorce may be reasonable. A therapist can help you sort through this dilemma.

Fact 5: The divorce takes place psychologically for children on the day of the separation.

The divorce occurs for children the day their parents separate. Visitation and placement schedules and support payments begin around that time, and the rules of the relationship also start changing with the separation. The legal divorce only solidifies those changes.

Fact 6: Two people living apart cannot live as cheaply as two people living together.

The first major reality of separation and divorce is financial. I'm sure that it's not news to you that two households are more costly to maintain than one. This can be a major problem for some families and can add to the stress and strain of divorce.

The financial impact of divorce on a family is several-fold, and much of the severity of it depends on the ages of your children. It may necessitate both parents working when before the divorce only one worked outside the home. Psychologically, children perceive this as a second loss (the first being when one parent moves out of the house).

4

The immediate financial impact is on short-term, daily finances. The crunch begins when attorneys ask for retainers of $1,000 to $5,000 or more just to begin a divorce action. Parents must turn to savings, if they have any, and in some cases they borrow against credit cards or from relatives.

Once a divorce action has begun, parents usually live in different places. They must pay two rents, or a mortgage and apartment rent, and two sets of utility, grocery, and insurance bills; their budget gets stretched to its limit or beyond. Many people living in one household are overextended, but if they must support two homes, they experience a tremendous change in essential versus nonessential expenses.

For children, a limited budget may mean a reduction in recreational activities and an end to ballet or karate lessons. They may have to wear clothes longer than before or wear hand-me-downs. Children may become bitter, resentful, disappointed, and unhappy. They may also have problems at school if they cannot dress to be socially acceptable or if they cannot attend school outings because of a fee that divorcing parents cannot afford.

Ironically, one of the common causes of divorce is financial irresponsibility on the part of one or both parents. If a parent is already financially irresponsible and his or her responsibilities increase because of divorce, the financial impact on the family is even greater.

When both parents are employed outside the home, the husband often makes more money than his wife, and this fact becomes a basic conflict in many divorces. One parent generally thinks the ex-spouse has the children too often, and the other parent thinks the ex-spouse has too much disposable income.

One of the long-term plans that is usually upset by divorce is saving for college. If a divorce drags on and involves many court appearances, you can spend the equivalent of several college educations. I was involved in one case in which, between the attorneys, psychologists, and other professionals, the couple spent $150,000. This kind of spending on a divorce angers children because they may be prevented from attending college or have to choose a less expensive school or forfeit going to a specialized school or one out of state.

It is not typical to read a divorce decree that has a plan for college expenses, because at 18 years of age a child is considered an adult and support payments stop. Also, it is difficult enough for attorneys and courts to agree on what should happen financially to an underage child. They don't want to plan for when a child becomes an adult, so in most divorce cases the college issue is ignored.

Fact 7: Two people living apart cannot see their children as often as two people living together.

Even in the most ideal situations, when parents live apart, they will have less access to their children than when they lived together. Typical visitation and placement schedules allow for a quarter to half time with each parent. That means you will be spending about three to six months less with your children each year.

Fact 8: Divorcing parents generally are upset by any extra time the other parent may have with the children.

Learn to value the time you have away from the children as much as the time you have with them. Save errands, doctor's appointments, and other personal business for when your children are with the other parent. This way, you will have more quality time with them, and you may actually be spending as much real time with your children as you did when they lived with you full-time.

Fact 9: Courts do not want to place children with a parent who is systematically trying to destroy the other parent.

Judges and court-appointed guardians are reluctant to place a child with a parent who feels the need to systematically destroy the other parent. Courts view such desire for destruction as a character flaw. Professionals believe one parent's desire to destroy the other also destroys that parent's ability to be a good role model for children. I heard a guardian say to a father, "Don't tell me the çhildren would be better off with you when your only purpose right now is to destroy their mother."

If you are in the heat of a custody dispute, step back and examine your actions.

- Are you keeping voluminous notes about every mistake the other parent makes?
- Do you call his or her neighbors, employers, coworkers, and relatives for negative information?
- Do you file motion after motion in court to discredit and denigrate the other parent?

If any of these patterns of behavior describe you, STOP. You are hurting yourself, your children, and your chances for reaching a good custody arrangement. If your spouse is that bad, he or she will demonstrate it through behavior. You will not have to prove anything.

Fact 10: Never ask a child to decide who he or she wants to live with.

Children are generally not concerned with who gets legal custody of them, but they are very concerned with where they will live. By involving a child in this decision, he or she is put under incredible pressure and in a no-win situation by being forced to accept one parent and reject the other. Often, one of the first things children ask is, "Who am I going to live with?" The answer is that they are likely to spend time with both parents, and the grown-ups will work out the details.

This concern is a big stressor for children. Imagine that as an adult you don't know where you are going to be living in three months, where you are going to work, where you will get your recreation and food, and if you are going to be able to see your friends. Even for an adult, this situation would produce great anxiety. Children live under that cloud for the entire period of a divorce and custody dispute.

Children who are especially worried will press the issue. As often as they ask where they are going to live is as often as parents have to stand firm and not incorporate children into this decision-making process. Most children under 15 years of age are incapable of making a fully informed decision about what living situation would be in their best interests. The younger they are, the more likely it is that their desires will be based on concrete matters, such as the size of a bedroom or the number of toys available.

Custody arrangements are something you and your spouse must try to work out. If you cannot come to a reasonable agreement about custody and visitation that is based on the welfare of your child and not your own desires, it will be up to the court with input from guardians and other professionals, such as psychologists, to make the decision for you.

Rarely will a court decide that a 16- or 17-year-old should live somewhere he or she doesn't want to, but in most cases the ultimate decision about custody and placement does rest with the courts. Young children simply need to know that you intend for them to be able to spend time with both of you. Teenagers need to know that their wishes will be considered as well.

A custody ruling appeal throws children right back into limbo until the appeal is heard. A child's underlying security is continually tested during custody battles.

Fact 11: You should be willing to do whatever you want your spouse to do.

Every new situation arising after the separation sets precedents or establishes new rules as to how things will continue. In establishing these rules, recognize that what's good for the goose is good for the gander and vice versa. Don't expect your spouse to do something that you are unwilling to do.

Fact 12: Unhappy mothers cannot raise happy children.

Although this issue cuts in both directions, because mothers receive placement in most cases, they are chosen as the descriptor in this rule. When a father continually undermines, sabotages, and makes life miserable for the mother, she will be very unhappy. Fathers must recognize that it is not possible for an unhappy mother to raise happy children. Therefore, fathers have a vested interest in keeping things on an even keel. The same is true if a father has custody and the mother is the potential saboteur.

Fact 13: Child support payments are intended to support your children, not to serve as extra spending money for your ex-spouse.

Too often a parent will say, "I'm not giving her a dime" or "I'm not giving him money to spend as he sees fit." It may be that not every dime from these payments is spent on supporting your children. Sometimes more money will be spent on the children than support provides and other times, less money is spent. In the end, however, it is your children who benefit from this money. Doing anything to directly or indirectly manipulate support payments affects your children. Do not use anger toward your ex-spouse as an excuse for manipulating support payments.

Fact 14: When parents live apart, children have more opportunities to manipulate them.

When parents live together, children try to take advantage of opportunities to manipulate one parent against the other. It's not unusual for a child to ask one parent if he or she can do something and after being told "no," to ask the other parent the same question. When parents live apart, they have more difficulty coordinating their answers, and therefore it becomes important for you to communicate effectively with one another to reduce manipulation.

Fact 15: "It is hard when children cannot spend time with someone they love."

This is a quote from a little girl who spoke it with tears running down her cheeks while I was seeing her in therapy. She said she still loved both her parents, but one parent was making it very difficult for her to see the other. In most cases, it is important for children to continue an ongoing relationship with both parents in spite of the anger the parents may feel toward each other.

Children may not be allowed to spend any time or only a small amount of time with the other parent for a number of reasons. They could include allegations that have been made, charges that have been filed, or extended periods of time when no contact was permitted. Even so, the parent with placement of the children must realize that the children probably still love the other parent and want to spend time with him or her.

Fact 16:   A parent should not become a peer and a child should not become a parent or peer.

It is such a big mistake when a parent tries to make a child his or her peer or tries to become a child's peer. Children generally have enough peers. They need parents to act like parents, not friends. A parent attempting to be a child's peer loses credibility when the need for discipline arises. Some parents try to compensate for the absence of the spouse by being more of a pal to their children, spending time playing with them, and doing things at the child's level. A parent taking on the role of a child's peer constitutes a change of rules that children don't always understand and that may be interpreted by them as inconsistency on the part of the parent.

Conversely, unless a parent handles the separation well, children may end up trying to parent the parent. They may respond to the unhappy parent by putting their arms around him or her to be consoling, assuring the parent that everything will be all right. Children actually say things like, "Don't worry. I'll always love you" or "You can talk to me about it."

The parent, needing support, may respond inappropriately to this attention by leaning on a child for emotional support, nurturance, and a sounding board for his or her feelings. Children then find themselves taking on the parent's worries and fretting about issues as an adult would. Suddenly, the child IS a parent and his or her childhood is stolen by being put into that position.

A variation of this occurs when parents turn their children into peers. Parents are accustomed to having each other to discuss ideas and ask for advice. Once the marital partner is no longer present or willing to participate in this exchange, the natural response is for the other partner to look for someone to fill the void. He or she often turns to those closest—the children—and this is another way of overburdening them. Drawing children into the decision-making process permeates all aspects of life, and they find themselves faced with questions about adult issues, such as: Should I date this man or woman? Should I spend this money now? Parents in the uncertain and frightening position of suddenly living alone with children must reassure them that even though the parents appreciate their love and attention, they are still children and must not try to take on adults' problems.

Fact 17: The more consistency parents provide in their children's lives, the healthier the children's adjustment will be.

Changes abound in a child's life during divorce. The more consistency you provide at this time, the more stable your child's life will be. When inconsistency is the order of the day, children will be less likely to adapt well to the divorce process.

Fact 18: The more flexibility a parent has regarding placement and visitation arrangements, the more comfortable children will be.

At the same time that you are trying to be consistent, you must also be flexible and "roll with the punches" as needed. For example, if Wednesday night is Mom's night with the children, but that night is a father/son activity at school, Mom should let the children go with Dad. Neither parent should say, "You can't have the kids because it's my night" when special activities are concerned.

Fact 19: Divorce is a process, not an event.

Too many people think of divorce only as the date on which the divorce actually occurs. Divorce is a process that begins when you first think about getting divorced, but doesn't end when you are done filing, mediating, and litigating. Situations such as children getting married and grandchildren being born will require you to deal with each other for the rest of your lives.

Fact 20: WINNING IS NEVER MORE IMPORTANT THAN THE WELL-BEING OF YOUR CHILDREN.

If you remember only one fact from this book, remember this: WINNING IS NEVER MORE IMPORTANT THAN THE WELL-BEING OF YOUR CHILDREN. No one wins a painful cus-

11

tody battle. In a custody dispute, it is not unusual for one parent to strongly believe that he or she is superior to the other parent, that the other parent is defective, and placement with the other parent would be detrimental for the children. However, there is a point of diminishing returns. When the pursuit of winning endangers the mental health of your children, you must step back and recognize that your children's well-being is more important than winning.

I am reminded of an attorney named Ted who, in the process of getting divorced, became obsessed with winning. Over the course of five years, he brought his ex-wife back to court three to four times a year, resulting in tens of thousands of dollars in legal fees for her. Almost every decision by the court was appealed and in several instances, Ted took issues to the state Supreme Court. He lost at every turn. He failed to recognize that his children were becoming more and more negatively affected by his behavior, and each child ended up in long-term psychotherapy to deal with Ted's behavior and with the fighting between their parents.

Ted also misperceived his children's anger toward him and thought his ex-wife had purposely turned the children against him, which caused him to believe that he needed to continue taking the issue to court. He actually alienated them himself by taking their mother to court so many times after the divorce.

Remember: WINNING IS NEVER MORE IMPORTANT THAN THE WELL-BEING OF YOUR CHILDREN.
WINNING IS NEVER MORE IMPORTANT THAN THE WELL-BEING OF YOUR CHILDREN.
WINNING IS NEVER MORE IMPORTANT THAN THE WELL-BEING OF YOUR CHILDREN.

Chapter

2

Moving Ahead: Telling Children about Your Divorce

With the facts from Chapter 1 in mind, and once you have your priorities in order, you can move ahead with the business of helping your children and yourself deal with the divorce process.

One of the most difficult things you will ever have to tell your children is that you are getting divorced. How you break this news to them makes a big difference in the magnitude of their fears and frustrations from the outset and in the apprehension with which the entire family approaches this major upheaval in their lives.

The ideal way to bring this very private matter between two people into a family forum is to make a formal announcement to your children, showing a unified front between you and your spouse. There are several things that you need to do and to keep in mind when telling your children about your divorce. These include:

- You and your spouse should be together when you break the news to your children. Regardless of how much acrimony exists between you, for that brief time it is very important for you to be able to put it aside so that your children see you together and recognize that this is something their parents (in spite of getting divorced) are able to work on together. It's also reassuring for children to see that you aren't coming apart at the seams while making this announcement.

- Give your children hugs and loving touches during this time, and hold their hands to be reassuring. You and your spouse don't need to touch each other, but you should both be affectionate toward your children.

- If you and your spouse cannot sit together to make this announcement without calling each other names or placing blame, each of you should meet separately with the children. In the absence of a visual unified front, however, you should at least decide together what you are going to tell the children so you can say the same thing.

- Whether you make the announcement together or separately, as part of your explanation for why you are divorcing you should avoid blaming each other and you should make sure your children don't think you are blaming them. Don't say, for example, "I'm divorcing your father because he's an alcoholic," or "I'm divorcing your mother because she's having an affair." This is not information children need to know and it will not be particularly useful in helping them understand the situation.

- If children ask why you are getting divorced, you can use carefully selected examples of what has been going on at home in your explanation. You might say: "You may have noticed that Mom and I have been arguing a lot lately and that we aren't sleeping in the same room anymore. That's because we aren't getting along as well as we used to, and we feel it might be better if we live apart instead of living together."

- What you say and how you phrase it depends on the ages of your children. Explanations to younger children should

14

be in simple, brief terms. You may tell them, "You've heard the word *divorce* and you see Mommy and Daddy living in different places. What we are doing is called getting divorced." Older children, who generally know what divorce means, usually want more information about why their parents can't stay together and what will happen next.

If a child asks, "Are you getting divorced because of Dad's (or Mom's) drinking?" obviously that's the message he or she has received. I always recommend that parents do not lie to their children. You can omit information, but you should not lie. If a child raises a point pertaining to an actual problem, such as a parent's drinking problem, there is nothing wrong with addressing it. You can say: "Obviously, you've noticed that this is a problem. It is part of our difficulties, but it is not the only problem."

- Another important message to give children is that even though you may have fallen out of love with each other, you will continue loving them. Explain the difference between the kind of love parents have for each other and the love they have for their children. One of the things children can be afraid of, which is not entirely illogical, is that you will stop loving them.

- Assure your children from the outset and over the course of time that they don't have to worry about details of the divorce. Tell younger children: "These are things the grown-ups are going to take care of, and we're going to try to let you just be children. You continue going to school and playing with your friends. We're going to watch things happen and figure it out in a way that's best for you."

- As best as you can in these early days of the divorce process, tell children what you expect to change and what you expect to remain constant. You might explain, "Dad (Mom) is going to find a new place to live," or "We're going to have to share the car because Mom (Dad) has to drive it to work and we'll only have it on the weekends."

- Avoid incorporating support or maintenance (alimony) issues into discussions with children. This can be very destructive to them. I'll explain more about that later.

15

Children also need to know that both parents are going to be taken care of during the divorce process. If you are following the most typical scenario, which is that Mom stays in the family house and Dad moves out as soon as is reasonable, the children should be shown where he is going to live so they can see that he has a bed to sleep in, a kitchen to eat in, and a bathroom. Children know how important these basic needs are and need to be sure that these needs are being met for both their parents.

If you have a family in which there are older and younger children, speak with them separately in addition to talking with them as a group, because what you tell a teenager, for example, is going to be different from what you tell a six-year-old.

Even though it is better to tell children about a divorce in a formal setting, they usually learn about divorce in an inappropriate way, either through your anger, communicated by things you say to them, or by being exposed to the hostilities that led to the divorce. For example, when putting your children to bed, you might say: "I don't want you to be surprised, so I'm telling you now that I'm filing for divorce tomorrow." Or you might blurt it out to your spouse in front of your children: "That's it. You've had it. We're getting that divorce." These types of statements have a devastating effect on children.

Most frequently, children overhear their parents shouting at one another late at night or when parents think the children are out of earshot, or they witness arguments that include the word divorce. Divorce adversely impacts all children. The extent to which it affects them, however, is based on their parents' behavior more than anything else. If children are trying to fall asleep and they hear their parents screaming in the living room—"I talked to my attorney today and I'm filing papers and you're going to be out of here before the weekend"—they can be traumatized, and the tone is set for the children to see how negative the divorce process is going to be.

Concrete Thinkers in an Abstract Situation

Regardless of how they have heard the news, once children understand that you are getting divorced, they will soon respond in a number of different ways, depending on their age. Let's divide children into three groups: early childhood (birth to age 6), middle childhood (6 to 12), and adolescents and older children (13 to 18).

Early Childhood

Children who are four years old or younger probably don't need to hear more than three or four simple sentences from you: "Your daddy and I are going to get divorced. This means we are going to live in different places. You will still spend time with both of us. We love you very much." They can't handle more than that. If they have questions, answer them as simply as possible.

Remember that actions speak louder than words, and all children, even very young ones, are going to react to what is happening in their environment. Your ability to handle your divorce in a relatively civil manner sends the message that life is going to be okay and not too much different than what they are accustomed to.

Hostility between you and your spouse causes instability in children in the early childhood group, and their immediate re-action will be crying and in many cases regressive behavior, such as bed-wetting, thumb-sucking, wanting to play with baby toys they haven't played with in a while, or not wanting to sleep without an overhead light. If the acrimony between you and your spouse continues, the disruptive behavior in young children will escalate.

Children under six also often experience feelings of guilt, thinking the divorce is their fault. They may say or believe things such as, "If I had been a better child, my parents would not be getting divorced."

Middle Childhood: Depression Becomes Anger with Age

To fully grasp reactions of the middle childhood group, you must understand that children don't start developing the capacity for abstract thinking until they are about 11 years old. This capacity is fully developed by about age 15. Issues such as love, falling out of love, and divorce have quite a few abstract aspects, which are lost on younger children.

The best example I can give of concrete versus abstract thinking is how an eight-year-old girl with whom I worked in therapy handled the concept of death. Coincidental to the therapy, the child's grandmother died. I asked how she felt about her grandmother's death and she said she was sad. I asked why she was sad and she replied: "Because now there won't be anybody to cut my hot dogs for me." She took the abstract concept of death and converted it into something concrete that she could understand.

Children in the younger end of the middle childhood group are likely to respond to news of a divorce with a depressive kind of behavior, becoming sullen, perhaps crying, and having reduced appetites. They may answer you in an indifferent, almost passive manner with "I don't care," and when asked what's bothering them, "nothing" may be a common reply.

They often react to divorce with feelings of sadness. What they had relied on as the family structure has collapsed, threatening their security. Emotional immaturity prevents them from protecting themselves against such losses, and because they have not yet developed the capacity for abstract thinking, they will not be able to process problems as they arise. This leads to greater sadness.

Emotional immaturity also means you cannot reassure these children that the loss of one parent does not automatically mean the loss of the other parent. Worrying about losing both parents through divorce is a source of genuine sadness and melancholy in children in this age group. I know of a nine-year-old girl named Vicki who had silently lived with this fear until it surfaced at a party. Vicki was dropped off at her friend's birthday party by her father, who promised to return at a certain time to take her home. As the party came to an end, parents picked up their children until Vicki was the only child left. Fearing that her father was not going to return, Vicki initially cried quietly, but as her fears mounted, she sobbed until she became hysterical. Her father was only 15 minutes late, but when he arrived, she blurted out: "I thought you had gone away and left me, just like Mommy left us."

Even if you try to explain these issues in an abstract way to children under 11 years of age, they will understand what you say in a concrete way.

Six-, seven-, and eight-year-olds tend to become very depressed about divorce because so many things change. They are saddened by Dad's car not being in the garage anymore, or by the basketball in the corner because he isn't there to play. They often pine for their fathers, because in most divorce cases the father leaves the household.

Some children in the middle childhood group feel hatred toward their parents, which they verbalize. They also experience almost uncontrollable anger and find concrete ways to apply that anger to the divorce situation. For example, a child who is intensely angry over his parents' divorce may say he is angry because his father, who has moved out and taken a weekend job to cover his additional expenses, can no longer take him to baseball practice on Saturdays and games on Sundays. He doesn't understand the subtleties of supporting two households and paying attorneys' fees and other costs associated with divorce. By the time the child is 15 years old, however, the anger dissipates because he understands the abstract elements of what has been going on.

As children get to be 9, 10, 11, and 12 years old, and sadness turns to anger, which can be manifested as rage and hate, they are apt to say spiteful, denegrating, hateful things to their parents and others. I worked with a 9-year-old boy and his brother and sister because a recommendation had been made to change their placement from their mother to their father. I started explaining to the children what was going to happen and why, and the 9-year-old looked at me with absolute fire in his eyes and said: "I hope you burn in hell for what you have done." This is the kind of hurtful thing children his age will say, and because of the level at which he was dealing with things, he meant it.

A parent can be overwhelmingly devastated to hear such a comment from his or her child. Parents take these statements very personally because they don't understand the dynamics of what is happening, and they feel hurt, guilty, and often depressed because they believe their children really feel this way.

19

It is vitally important to help a child deal with and diffuse these angry feelings. If these feelings are not resolved, the child may have serious relationship problems as an adult. A parent may be tempted to take advantage of a child's angry feelings toward the other parent, creating an alliance that may make the parent feel triumphant. This, however, is divisive and prevents a child from resolving his or her anger and moving on. Unfortunately, when a parent uses this kind of anger to form an alliance with a child, the situation often backfires during adolescence and may culminate in even greater anger against the divisive parent.

Loyalty issues frequently develop during this period. Children come to rely most on the parent who remains at home, seeing him or her as the key provider upon whom they are dependent for all basic needs. Even if that parent is not the principal financial provider, because he or she is in the homestead, the child's perception is that primary allegiance belongs with that parent.

If that parent is angry with the other, a child tends to take sides and generally feels it is safer to identify with the parent who provides all these benefits. A child will almost always manifest this loyalty without explaining it in terms of personal security, something that he or she may not even recognize as the motivation. Instead, it generally appears like this:

Bobby comes home from a visit with his father saying, "I don't want to visit Dad anymore." His mother, Marjorie, presumes her son has recognized what a wretch his father is, and she tells him: "I can understand why you don't want to visit with him. If you don't want to go anymore, you don't have to." Marjorie now feels that she has an ally in her son and will continue to bad-mouth his father and not support or encourage visitation.

Regardless of how she feels about her ex-husband, Marjorie should put Bobby's needs to have a positive, loving relationship with both parents before her own needs to vent and form alliances. The scenario should have gone like this:

Bobby comes home from visiting his father and says he doesn't want to go there anymore. If this is the first time he has said this, Marjorie should question his reasons. Has his father mistreated him, offended him, or done something else to alienate him?

If the answers to those questions are yes, there may be a legitimate reason to stop supporting or even allowing visitation. However, if Bobby is vague and says something like, "It's not fun being with him," Marjorie should say, "I can understand that you might have more fun here. However, he is your father, he loves you, and wants to spend time with you. The way he and I feel about each other should have nothing to do with your relationship with your father."

She should also add, "If things aren't going as well as you would like when you visit your father, maybe we should all sit down and discuss it so we can make things better." This position is difficult to take if you are angry with your spouse, in the throes of divorce, and perhaps even fighting for custody. However, it is the best one to take for the child's benefit, and you may even quell some of your own anger by having to focus on being so reasonable and rational.

Marjorie's first response illustrates the type of highly destructive reaction that will interfere with a child's ability to establish appropriate relationships in adolescence and early adulthood. The second type of response, however, will lead to more positive outcomes and better adjustment.

Straddling Two Worlds: The Struggle for Teenage Independence

It is easy to forget in the turmoil of divorce that children are dealing not only with the emotional upheaval and problems associated with their parents' lives, but with changes they undergo as they mature. This is perhaps best illustrated in teenagers.

When children reach their teenage years they need to start separating from their parents. Look at typical adolescent development and you will see that as time goes on teenagers want to spend less and less time with their parents and more and more time with their friends. They begin to straddle the worlds of childhood and adulthood, dealing with a host of emotional and physical changes, as well as challenges presented by a higher level of education. Parents too often misunderstand what is happening through normal development, and they misinterpret their teenagers' desire to separate from the family as having to do with the divorce.

If a divorce is taking place, teenagers generally want to be even more separate from their families. I recall one situation involving two girls, ages 16 and 18. When the divorce started, they were 14 and 16 years old and the older child was knee-deep in the fight. By the time the divorce finally took place, she was almost 18 and she basically blew it off, saying: "I don't care what you people do. I'm going to college and I don't want to have anything to do with this anymore. I've got my own life."

A different kind of anger develops in teenagers than in the young and middle childhood groups. To understand it, think of the Greek term *sophomore*, which means wise fool. We often accuse high school and early college students of having sophomoric attitudes and a sophomoric way of thinking. A high school sophomore is typically 15 going on 16 years old and has just developed the ability to think in the abstract. These teenagers generally figure they have solved the problems of the world and no one can tell them anything they don't know.

At this age, they use their abilities to reflect back on what happened when they were 9 and 10 years old. Assume that during that period of time, much of the anger they had for their parents was based on one parent saying negative things about the other, doing negative things, subverting the visitation schedule, alienating a child from the other parent. Now the child is a teenager and reasons, "I see what Mom (Dad) was doing all that time and it wasn't nice." Now the teenager becomes angry with one or both parents.

Teenagers generally have no compunctions about saying to a parent, "You ruined my childhood with my father (mother) by doing these things and I don't want to have anything to do with you because of that." Their anger takes on a different form and sometimes adds to a teenager not wanting to spend time with one or the other parent.

Adolescents are also subject to a kind of pseudomaturity, caused when teenagers become parentified. As I described earlier, this happens when one parent turns a teenager into a parent (this also occurs in intact families) through the nature of responsibilities and demands made on the child. This pseudomaturity robs childhoods, adds to anxiety and depression, and can also increase the level of anger a teenager feels toward his or her parents.

Despite their roller-coaster ride to maturity, teenage children have an easier time with divorce than do younger children because they have already begun to become independent. However, when telling teenagers about your divorce, remember that trust is important to them and you must be totally honest about why the marriage has not worked out.

If the divorce is the result of extramarital affairs, alcoholism, mental illness, or abuse, teenagers may be told—but spare them the gruesome details. If they suspect any of these issues were problems, they will be relieved to know their perceptions were accurate.

Discussions with teenage children about relationships are very important at this time. When teenagers emerge from divorce feeling that personal relationships are not worth the effort, their own meaningful relationships may be disrupted in the future.

You must help teenagers realize that problems in the marriage were related to the relationship between two specific people, and that not all relationships need to be that way. This concept is sometimes difficult for young people to grasp because children judge all behavior and what is considered acceptable against what happens in their own homes. The way couples communicate or don't, the way they speak to each other, and the manner in which they treat their children are learned at home.

One of the best ways to convey to teenagers that all relationships are not supposed to be disappointing and tumultuous is by saying, "What you see happening at home is not the way life is supposed to be between two people who love and respect each other. They are not supposed to lie to each other, hit each other, or cheat on each other." You can add, "Learn what not to do in a relationship by watching what your father (mother) and I are going through. Don't become bitter or jaded."

Another approach to help reduce the impact of negative parental behavior associated with divorce is by asking your teenager to envision how the relationship between his or her parents should be. You can start by saying: "You know the things your father (mother) and I are doing wrong. It's not difficult to see how they affect both of us and you." Then use specific examples to start an exchange between you and your teenager. "Your father and I spend a lot of time screaming at each other. How do you think couples should commmunciate?"

This type of communication between you and your teenagers demands that you calm down and focus. If you also have younger children, you may find them joining in at their own level, asking questions and looking to you to help them figure it out. You may actually need some counseling from an objective observer, such as a therapist, to be able to deal with your children on this level, especially if you are in the midst of a super-charged divorce and custody case.

When Your Child Is No Longer a Child

I have already mentioned how divorce can wipe out college plans. However, older children confront more than questions about who will pay for higher education once their parents are divorced. To begin with, people erroneously believe that because college-age children are considered adults, divorce will not seriously impact them. This is not true.

The 20s are an age when children completely separate from their parents and start displaying distinctive characteristics that make them individuals. College-age students are only beginning to identify these traits, and although their bodies and minds are fully developed, they still have not developed a true sense of who they are apart from their families.

While college-age children search for their own identities, they are employing some of that sophomoric thinking I talked about earlier. Consequently, they are more likely to blame one parent or the other for the failure of the marriage instead of recognizing that two people were involved in the process. They also tend to choose sides, having a difficult time establishing a sense of independence from both parents.

Tolerance and patience are just as crucial for dealing with children in this age group as in any other. Here are some guidelines:

- Both parents should discourage college-age children from choosing sides. Remind them that they are no longer little children and that they should be able to look at the entire picture objectively.

- Continue to avoid dirty details of where the marriage went wrong and why the divorce was unpleasant. Talk in general about the reasons for the failed relationship and the roles both of you played in it.

- It is very important, once again, for both parents to be saying the same thing. If you are blaming each other, your child will end up acting as judge and jury, weighing the evidence and deciding who was right and who was wrong. Don't give your child that kind of power over your life, and don't inflict that kind of burden on him or her.

- When dealing with adult children, you can talk more about your personal emotional turmoil and how you felt about ending a marriage, thereby making yourself more of a real person and less of a parent who wounded his or her children and destroyed the family by getting divorced.

- If something as identifiable as alcoholism, adultery, abandonment, or abuse led to the divorce, say so, but don't do it as a way of placing blame. Don't say: "Your father was nothing but a drunk who couldn't support the family. He left me no choice but to throw him out." Do say: "Your father was an alcoholic who refused to recognize his disease and get help. I did my best to live with him, but I finally realized that I could not help him and it was better for all of us if he stopped living with us and he and I divorced."

- Always tell the truth to adult children, but be concise and kind in your delivery. Hammering an adult child with the faults of the other parent serves no good purpose and if it affects the way he or she feels or thinks about that parent, the child may eventually resent you, too, for having triggered those negative feelings.

Boys and Girls React Differently

Just as different age groups exhibit different reactions to divorce, likewise there are differences between the way boys and girls react to the dissolution of their parents' marriage. Initially, boys are more negatively affected by divorce than are girls, and sometimes for longer periods of time. They act out more in school, have more trouble with relationships, and display longer lasting, sometimes more dramatic, poor school performance.

Some traditional stereotypes creep into the way boys and girls see themselves in a divorce situation. These influences may be acquired through parental behavior, entertainment, reading materials, school, and friends and their families. In families where two parents are present, boys tend to feel greater responsibility for the stability of the household and family than do girls. Girls tend to be more nurturing, often assuming caretaker/giver roles within the family.

During a divorce, boys tend to want to assume responsibility for the family in Dad's absence, even to the point where they may get part-time jobs to help support the family. Girls tend to see themselves as the emotional glue, and during a divorce they bury or deny their own feelings while being more concerned about the family's moral and ethical fiber and about other people's feelings. Girls sometimes appear to be taking their parents' divorces better than boys, but looks can be deceiving.

Later on, girls' relationships seem to suffer more from the effects of their parents' divorces than do boys' relationships. Many women with divorced parents tend to marry and divorce early; they may become promiscuous and may have difficulty trusting their partners, heterosexual or homosexual. Girls of divorced parents also tend to have more problems with heterosexual relationships, with instability and abuse being among the major difficulties.

26

Here again, speaking with your children, getting them to examine and verbalize their feelings, and being as positive as possible about your love for them and their continued relationship with both parents are very effective methods in helping children deal with divorce.

Adjustments Abound

The adjustment period to divorce lasts 6 to 12 months after the divorce is final under the best circumstances, and is critical for parents and children as they deal with such concerns as:

- Becoming accustomed to new relationships.
- Becoming familiar with visitation schedules.
- Moving to a new neighborhood.
- Going to a new school or job.

Most children are able to make the necessary adjustments to cope with changes precipitated by divorce. Societal issues vary from situation to situation, depending on the reason for the divorce, the home environment prior to it, how lengthy the process is and, as I've said, a child's age.

To help children adjust, you must be aware of the various areas of their lives that are affected by divorce. Be alert to changes in their:

- Level of play, to the point where they may not want to play, choosing instead to mope around the house or hang around the parent who is present. They may not want to socialize with friends, opting instead to spend more time playing "alone" games. They may avoid games requiring a fair amount of attention and interaction because they are worried about their home life and cannot properly focus.

- Interaction with friends. They may become hostile, even picking fights with children with whom they had been friendly. They may lose interest in established friendships, or hang out on the periphery of a group of friends, feeling

27

and playing the role of outsider or outcast. They may gravitate toward a new, less desirable set of friends, perhaps children from divorced households or children who are rougher and appear more hardened toward life.

• Physical health. They may become more susceptible to illness. Children who are unhappy and run down and not eating or sleeping properly because of the situation at home tend to be ill more often with colds, headaches, and more serious illnesses such as depression.

• School performance, which is also a barometer of how your children are being impacted by divorce. All children's schoolwork generally suffers immediately after separation or divorce and during custody battles. Declines in grades and lack of interest at school can continue for two to three years and longer after a divorce is final.

Look for these signs that the upheaval at home is spilling over into school, and don't wait to act:

• Your child starts coming home without books, homework, or both, and makes lame excuses. Call his or her teacher and ask about homework and your child's performance in general. Explain your concern and if you have not already told the school about your divorce, you may do so. However, spare teachers and school officials unpleasant details unless they absolutely need to know something specific.

• Work that is generally neat and complete becomes sloppy and incomplete. Again, phone or visit the school.

• Study time is spent daydreaming, there is resistance to studying that did not exist before the divorce, or your child is spending as much time studying as in the past but cannot remember anything. These are signs of a preoccupied mind, and your child may need therapy or to be in a support group. Some schools have support groups for children of divorced parents.

Mourning the End of a Marriage

In addition to all these reactions, divorce presents a host of emotional changes that occur again and again in the form of a grief cycle, affecting children and adults. Most couples generally feel a tremendous sense of loss when their marriage ends, even if both spouses wanted to divorce. When one parent did not want a divorce, however, he or she mourns the end of that marriage, experiencing the same grief that occurs after the death of a loved one.

The grief cycle encompasses:

- Sadness or depression, at times bordering on being debilitating because of its potential to be overwhelming.

- Anger over the loss, sometimes with the person who has moved out, and sometimes with oneself for having allowed the loss to take place or for being unable to have seen it coming.

- Resignation and a resolution to go on despite the loss.

A person in a divorce situation is continually reminded of the lost relationship because the other parent is still alive and serves as a reminder of what is gone. As a parent in the throes of divorce, you must deal with all of this while being there for your children, trying to understand their feelings, and helping them cope with their own grief.

The grief children experience in divorce is different from what their parents undergo. Even though they may not fully understand the abstract concept of death, children realize that when a loved one dies, he or she is not coming back to see them, hassle them, or do things with them. However, most children generally expect to see both parents after a divorce, so they do not have the sense of finality associated with death.

Children grieve the parent who moves out and the reduced interaction with him or her. They are also upset over less interaction with the parent that stays if he or she is home less because of working extra hours or extra jobs and over the violation of the

29

family unit and consequent loss of activities as a family. Because of these feelings, a child who cannot access you immediately when he or she needs or wants you perceives this inaccessibility as another loss and engages in a mini-grieving process.

Allow your child to call the other parent or volunteer to drive him or her to see that parent. Don't be negative by saying, "It's too late (or too early) to call" or "You already called your dad (mom) today, so you can't call again" or "You know how much I hate it when you call him (her)." If you respond in an unreasonable fashion, a child may grow sadder and more depressed.

The grief cycle occurs repeatedly for parents and children, coming into play anytime a situation arises in which the parent wishes he or she were still married. For example, if Mom goes to school for open house and the teacher talks about a project that fathers can work on with their children and there's no father around, Mom is given an opportunity to resume her grief cycle. She becomes sad and angry, but then reaches a resolution. In this case, her resolution may be to do the project herself with her child, or to ask her ex-spouse or a male relative to do it.

Every milestone that a child reaches where it would be important for the missing parent to be present or participating may trigger grief. This situation is particularly true with adolescents because, whether their families are intact or broken, they usually gravitate toward the same-gender parent. Boys are turning into men and girls are becoming women and they are looking for someone to emulate and turn to for advice and approval.

In the divorcing family, this becomes more problematic for a teenager living with a parent of the opposite gender. The child must make due with whatever that parent has to offer, which may not be enough to fill his or her needs. Under these circumstances, a child may ask to live with the same-gender parent. This doesn't stem from hatred or dissatisfaction, but from a basic need to live with someone with whom he or she has more in common. It is very difficult to let a child go under such circumstances and equally challenging not to take it personally, but it must be done if the other parent is willing and capable of properly caring for the child. If the move is not possible, your teenager is apt to experience more grief.

Certain behavioral reactions to grief may be anticipated in children based on their ages. Very young children generally experience more confusion than actual grief when one parent is suddenly missing. Children between the ages of 6 and 8 are apt to do a lot of crying and become depressed. Children between the ages of 9 and 12 often experience agitated depression, which looks more like anger than depression and may be mistaken for acting out angry behavior.

The Challenge of Role Reversal

All the while that children and parents are dealing with waves of grief, they must also meet other challenges to their emotional stability, including a reversal of roles in parents. In scenarios, for example, where the father moves out and the mother takes on all responsibility for the home, children may see her performing tasks that were previously carried out by their father, such as shoveling snow or making household repairs. When children visit their father, they may see him doing things he had not done when the family was together, such as laundry, ironing, cooking, or arranging a schedule for his children.

In one sense, a reversal of roles is not bad, because I believe adults should be viewed equally and children should see their parents sharing responsibilities. Role reversal becomes a problem for adults and children, however, when suddenly one parent is absent and the task of keeping the home and family organized and operating as close to normal as possible (normal is the operative word) becomes much more difficult. With a change in roles comes a change in the frustration level of the parents, which affects the children. As I have said, if you don't have a happy parent, you don't have happy children. Children end up modeling the sadness, depression, or inappropriate expressions of anger that they see in their parents.

31

Not Enough Hours in the Day, Not Enough Friends in the World

Another major stressor for adults and children that occurs after one parent moves out—a stressor that is directly related to role reversal—is time or the lack of it. All players in the family find themselves dealing with the feeling that their world has been turned upside down, and rules that were in place in the household are gone. They realize that things they had done together or worked on as a team are now left to one person.

Intact families in which responsibilities fall mostly to one parent because the other is not around to help as much as would be desirable do not experience as much change when divorce occurs as do families in which parents had worked more cooperatively. When change is sudden and the time stressor strikes, the parent with all the responsibility feels overwhelmed: he or she has to get up at 5 A.M., is not finished until 1 A.M., has no time to sleep or read or look at a videotape, and then has to start all over again. This parent needs recreation, but generally has no time for it, not even enough money not even to go bowling or to a movie, especially because the children require even more attention than they did before the divorce.

The more frustrated you become, the more aggressive you are likely to be. Physically inappropriate behavior toward children tends to increase at these times and sometimes escalates to child abuse. Children tend to get hit more by divorced parents than by nondivorced parents.

Another major stressor is social relationships. Although you may need a night out, even if you have the disposable income, you may not be inclined to go because you may have to recreate alone. Most friends prior to the divorce choose sides with one parent or the other in divorces. A divorcing couple will rarely be able to both remain friends with the same people. It is almost as if the parents are fighting for custody of their friends as well as of their children. A woman, for example, may find herself alienated from a neighborhood friend whose husband has chosen her ex-spouse's side in the divorce. Or, she may find herself isolated from married friends because she is suddenly perceived as being lonely, emotionally needy, and available. Suddenly, people she thought she would be able to rely on for social support are gone, and she experiences another loss.

Be sure you have an appropriate support network during this time, even if it is composed only of relatives and/or friends at work. Be on the alert, however, for deserters from the ranks of your relatives, particularly grandparents and in-laws, which is another big social stressor and yet another loss. In spite of what may have gone on in the home, grandparents tend to ally themselves with their natural child against a son-in-law or daughter-in-law.

The divorce process is really a series of losses—personal, social, or financial—and related grief.

One Magical Wish

Through all this confusion, sadness, and insecurity, children often carry with them, even into adulthood, the wish that their parents will magically be reunited. One of the questions I ask children during custody evaluations is: "If you had three wishes, what would they be?" Most of them wish their parents would get back together. This wish does not die when parents remarry. It often continues well beyond the time of the divorce and even after remarriage, and stems from children's longing for life to return to the simpler way it was prior to the divorce.

I don't think the shock of divorce ever wears off children, which is one reason many of them cling to this dream long after it is clear to others that such an outcome is impossible. Because of this wish, children, including adult children, may unknowingly or knowingly interfere with parents establishing new relationships. Some children feel so strongly about this and act out such negative behavior against a parent's new partner that people actually forego remarriage.

It takes an extraordinary amount of tact and courage to deal with this situation. You do not want to alienate your children or create a hostile, intolerable environment that will end in another divorce, but at the same time you don't want to deny yourself a new, positive relationship and marriage. In some cases, children never come around, but a percentage of them accept, if not ultimately embrace, stepparents if they are provided with a happy, peaceful, and fulfilling environment. (I'll talk more about this later.)

It isn't easy to try to create new beginnings when your children must be your primary concern. Nothing about divorce is easy. Divorce when children are concerned can be hell.

▼

Chapter

3

Custody Options: The Best Interest of the Child

Coming to terms with certain facts about divorce and its impact on you and your children is crucial if you are going to move through the custody process with any degree of levelheadedness and right thinking.

By the time you find yourself dealing with custody issues, you will have addressed the initial questions about what life is apt to bring for you and your children in the immediate future and the things that are probably going to unfold in your home in the short term. Once your life stabilizes a bit (provided you are not dealing with radical concerns such as family violence, physical or sexual abuse, or alcohol or drug use), you will be confronted with the issue of where your children are going to live and who is going to be responsible for what happens in their daily lives, including such basic tasks as buying their clothes, taking them to the doctor, and attending school conferences.

More importantly, you will have to decide if they are going to live with one parent all the time and visit the other parent some of the time or if you are going to divide their time evenly between both of you. Initially, most parents take an emotional stand, wanting their children with them all the time. They might acknowledge that their ex-spouse has legal rights, but they still want the children to themselves. They also confuse custody and placement.

Many parents at this point in the divorce and custody process don't realize the difference between custody and placement. Custody generally refers to who has decision-making power over the children. It identifies who has legal rights, and not necessarily where the children will be living. Placement refers to the amount of time children will spend with each parent—or with whom they will live.

When deciding placement schedules, you must also realize that there are financial considerations. A primary placement parent generally will receive support from the other parent, and placement of the children may also determine who keeps the family homestead. These are decisions that can be made between parents, with the help of attorneys, through mediation, or, ultimately, by the court.

The process was more restrictive in the past. It was common practice in the 1800s for the father to be given custody of the children. Children were considered property and women were not allowed to own property. During the Industrial Revolution, people began recognizing the important nurturing bonds that develop between mothers and children, and the pendulum swung in the opposite direction. It was then widely believed that fathers did not have the capacity to be sensitive, or to nurture and care for children. The "tender years doctrine" was born and, for a number of years, mothers generally received placement of their children.

In the late 1960s and early 1970s, a new concept, known as "best interest," evolved, allowing children to be placed with the parent who represented their best interests. This meant that mothers and fathers theoretically were playing on a level field, with each having an equal chance of receiving placement of their children.

In 1979, the Uniform Marriage and Divorce Act identified many factors that should be addressed when considering the best interests of children. Today, children are placed with their mothers in most cases after divorce and in more than half of the cases when there is a custody dispute. One reason for this is that fewer mothers than fathers work full-time, so mothers are usually more available to care for their children than are fathers. This is not to suggest that one gender is superior or inferior to the other regarding child-rearing skills.

Joint versus Sole Custody

You must decide if you want to ask the court for joint or sole custody of your children and which of you will have primary placement. A number of factors should be kept in mind when considering this decision.

In joint custody situations, parents have joint legal rights. To make joint custody work, you and your spouse must be able to communicate well enough with one another to make joint decisions about such things as your children's education, nonemergency medical treatment, religious upbringing, marriage before the legal age, and early enlistment in the armed forces. Bear in mind as you work out this issue that visitation schedules, child support, and the overall mental health of all concerned are normally better in joint custody situations.

However, if a divorce has been so messy that parents cannot work together, sole custody may be the better route. Under sole custody arrangements, major life decisions do not have to be cleared with the former spouse, although the parent who is assigned sole custody needs to be mindful of the child's need to have a relationship with the other parent. One of the problems that arises with sole custody is that it suggests ownership to the parent who has custody. When a custodial parent acts as if he or she owns the children, the other parent may feel excluded and stop visiting them or even stop making child support payments.

Because of this sense of ownership and the isolation of the other parent, courts and psychologists who evaluate children in divorce situations recommend joint custody most of the time. The thinking is that under such arrangements, parents are presumably more satisfied and children benefit from having regular input from both parents in decisions that affect their lives. For example, if children are going to change from parochial to public school, or if a child needs corrective surgery, parents should make these decisions together. As new situations arise in children's lives, it is usually better if both parents are involved in the decision-making process. This involvement does not always happen in joint custody situations, but it is the goal.

A key issue to consider when deciding whether to pursue sole custody is that the custodial parent will be required to take on full responsibility for the children—there is no vacation from decision making, no partner, even if it is a former spouse, to share the burden. This task is an enormous one to shoulder alone, which is why joint custody is an attractive alternative for many parents.

Although parents usually have a choice about whether to seek joint or sole custody, some situations indicate the need for sole custody. You should definitely pursue sole custody if your former spouse:

- Is chronically mentally ill.

- Is an active alcoholic.

- Has a history of physical abuse.

- Has a history of sexual abuse.

- Continually undermines the children's relationship with the other parent.

- Continually violates court orders.

- Refuses to communicate effectively with the other parent.

- Actively obstructs visitation.

- Uses poor judgment in child care.

- Engages in behaviors dangerous to the children.

Chronic Mental Illness Leads to a Topsy-Turvy World

Being with a parent who is suffering from chronic mental illness wreaks havoc on children because it keeps them off balance, endangers their physical and mental well-being, and actually terrorizes them. One case I've had involving mental illness was like a double-edged sword. The mother, a teacher whom I'll call Ellen, came from a dysfunctional family from which she was anxious to flee. She married a businessman, Robert, who she thought was going to be her knight in shining armor and rescuer. The fantasy held up for about five years and then they had four daughters. Robert became a senior executive and spent a lot of time traveling so most of the responsibilities at home fell to Ellen.

Managing her home and children became a dreadful burden for her. As the magic began to fade from her marriage, Ellen started coming apart at the seams. She became unable to deal with Robert's absence and began losing her ability to handle even typical daily stress. Normal psychological defenses, such as crying and sleep, failed her, and Ellen developed a number of symptoms to distance herself from the situation at home, including abnormal anger with her husband and losing touch with reality. Ellen had to be admitted to a hospital, where she was given medication and told to go into therapy.

Robert eventually filed for divorce, and during the process it was discovered that he had a substance abuse problem. The children, who ranged in age from 6 to 13, found themselves dealing with the first two situations on the list of cautions mentioned earlier—Mom with one and Dad with the other. The court said that because of Robert's substance abuse problems, Ellen should have the children. But Robert went into treatment under court supervision that included random urine screens, and he started recovering.

Ellen, because of her anger with Robert, would not let his substance abuse problems fade into his background. Even after their divorce, she continued telling everyone they knew about his drug abuse, including teachers at the school attended by their daughter Sandy, putting that child in an embarrassing and awkward position. Ellen, often still out of touch with reality, frequently called another daughter, Kelly, by Robert's girlfriend's name, ranting: "You're not Kelly, you're Laurie, and all you want is to get me out of the picture." When Kelly would ask her mother why she called her Laurie, Ellen would deny having done so, clearly unaware of her actions.

When the children were brought to me for counseling, they cried because they didn't understand what their mother was doing. They had no stability at home because from one minute to the next they couldn't predict if their mother was going to call them names, throw things at them, scream at them, or not recognize them. At one point, Ellen flew to Arizona, never telling Robert about the trip, and the children came home from school to an empty house. Mindy, the youngest of the girls, stood on the front stoop crying uncontrollably because she didn't know where her mother was and thought no one was home was because the house was on fire.

As a result of what they were being subjected to by their mother, the children started losing touch with reality, behaving irrationally, and regressing, doing things too young for their years. Mindy, for example, would sit in my office chewing tissues, then sticking the wet paper on her body or spitting it on the floor. Jane, another daughter, would sit in my office staring at her hands as she made strange movements with them. Sandy would sit with tears streaming down her face, saying: "You've got to do something about this. When can I get out of there?"

Robert, who was deeply concerned about what was happening, won from the court an emergency transfer placement and moved his daughters to his home. The morning after the transfer took place, an angry Ellen telephoned the children, yelling at them, calling them names, and blaming the entire situation on them. "I don't know what you said," Ellen shouted into the phone, "but whatever you told everyone, you made this happen. It's all your fault." The children were devastated by what she said, and they became confused and anxious because they didn't understand what they had done wrong.

A short time after their transfer, however, the girls seemed very happy, and when they came to my office they gave me a spontaneous concert, singing songs they had been taught by their father and his wife. It's difficult to describe the joy I felt watching them as they sang. They were relaxed, teasing and poking fun at each other and chasing each other around the room. This was in complete contrast to how they acted around their mother, when they were always on their guard, waiting and wondering what was going to happen next.

Ellen had been granted supervised visitation, but after her disruptive phone calls, she dropped out of contact with the children. As this case illustrates, from a custody evaluation standpoint, children should be kept away from chronically mentally ill parents.

Active Alcoholism or Other Drug Abuse and Children Don't Mix

The problems experienced with alcoholics are in many ways similiar to what happens with parents who are chronically mentally ill. One of the major concerns is the lack of predictability, which leaves children off balance and always cautious and fearful, just as in Ellen and Robert's case. They wonder: "Is Dad (Mom) going to be drunk tonight, and if he (she) is drunk, is it going to be a happy drunk, a sad drunk, or a mad drunk?"

Alcoholics, like mentally ill persons such as Ellen, slip in and out of psychotic-like episodes and don't remember what they did when they were drunk. Many children who have been abused say their fathers, mothers, or both parents were abusive only when drunk. This is highly credible because alcohol reduces a person's ability to control his or her impulses.

Another problem for alcoholics is DENIAL. They put so much energy into denying the existence of a problem that they can't recognize its seriousness. Alcoholics' denial systems are so strong that they don't realize when they are losing their marriages, children, or jobs. If they can't recognize something so involved

41

and important, how are they going to tend to the day-to-day needs of their children? A recent national survey of more than 200 psychologists reports that the number one reason for granting sole custody to a parent was that the other parent was an alcoholic.

Physical or Sexual Abuse: Confounding Dilemmas

The rule is the same for physical or sexual abuse: If you do this to your children, you forfeit the right to be involved in decisions that affect their lives. This is clearly for the protection of the children because people who have sexually abused youngsters may stop and not do it for years and then start all over again, and that's very scary. The notion that we no longer have to worry about an abuser who has been in therapy for a few years is not necessarily valid.

Sexual abuse is another confounding dilemma for children. If a child has been sexually abused by a parent, that doesn't mean the parent doesn't love the child and the child doesn't love the parent. It also doesn't mean that the parent hasn't taken the child to a zoo or a park or taught him or her to shoot baskets or ride a bike. Children like to capture good memories, such as outings or being taught fun things, and then try to resurrect the relationship with the parent(s) without the abusive component. The hope that this can be accomplished may make some children reluctant to report abuse. Another problem in dealing with abused children, and one reason why abuse may go unrecognized for a long time, is that children rarely tell the whole story at once. They usually send up a trial balloon to see how it is received. If it is received by an adult with an open mind, they tell more. If it is not, they generally don't. Once the abuse is known, however, a child cannot be left in that situation under any circumstances.

42

Violating Orders, Communication Failure, Obstructing Visits

I consider parents who continually violate court orders, refuse to communicate with the other parent, and actively obstruct visitation, to be problem parents. By violating court orders or obstructing visits, they are undermining their children's relationship with the other parent. And by refusing to communicate effectively with the other parent, they are causing problems. I recommend couples therapy for parents who are getting divorced or who have gotten divorced probably as frequently as I do for married couples, because parents have to be able to communicate effectively with one another.

If you have a situation in which you continually try to get the other parent into therapy but he or she storms out or otherwise subverts the process, the basic message is that this parent does not want to make it as easy as possible for the children. The lack of communication will manifest itself in other areas and the children's relationship with the other parent will be undermined as one parent becomes more and more manipulative.

Many different actions can constitute a violation of court orders. Perhaps a mother is told by the court that she can visit her children but her boyfriend cannot be present because he has a criminal record, so she tries to include the boyfriend without anyone learning about it. Or a father keeps showing up for his assigned visitations but the mother isn't there with the children when she is supposed to be. Or a father is supposed to bring the children home to his former spouse at a particular time and day but he brings them back whenever he pleases. The parent who is willing to disregard judicial authority and do whatever he or she pleases is not going to listen to what another parent says.

Parents may not realize that by doing such spiteful things, they are negatively affecting their children. Invariably at the holidays I get calls from parents who are supposed to start visitation at a particular time and place but the former spouse presents a conflict. I was involved with one family at Christmastime one year when the mother wanted to take her son to visit his grandparents

43

in Florida. She asked her former husband if she could have the child the night before because the only flight she could get was especially early the next day. The father, who was a control freak, did not want to give the child to her the night before because it wasn't her visitation time. He promised to bring the child to the airport on time the next day.

The mother was at the airport when her ex-husband showed up, without the child, with the excuse that his mother had taken the child somewhere and he did not know where. We later learned that the child had been at home with Grandma all the while and the father was just harrassing his ex-wife. She lost their tickets and had to pay full price for another flight the next day, and the child was caught in the middle of a lie told by his father. This situation is terrible for a child. Obstructing visits is another area in which parents can be so manipulative that children cannot predict their actions.

Endangering Your Children

Parents who use poor judgment in child care and whose behavior endangers their children are clearly incapable of making proper decisions for the children and should not share custody. This includes, for example, parents who take their children to bars. They don't want to find or pay for a babysitter so they take their youngsters to bars and stay out as late as they choose. In one case, a father put his five-year-old daughter on a table at a bar and had the child perform so he could get free drinks from other patrons. Also, parents who drink and drive with their children in the car are endangering their children.

The problem is not only that these parents are endangering their children's physical well-being but also that children learn what they live. The basic message children learn from this type of behavior is that it is appropriate. These children are also more likely to grow up to be alcoholics than are other children. Such actions distort their value system and cheapen their dignity and sense of self-worth. What do these children learn from being taken to a meat-market-type bar where they can watch people grope each other or get staggering drunk? Worse yet, what do these children learn if one of the people being watched is their parent?

There's a long list of behaviors that are considered to be in poor judgment. For example, when is it appropriate to leave a child alone? Laws in some states say this is okay to do when a child is 11 or 12 years old, but does that mean every night? Does that mean all night? I had a case in which a five-year-old boy was proud to demonstrate in my office what his mother, who often left her children alone, had taught him to do to save his three-year-old sister if there was a fire in their house. Children are left alone thousands of times a day around the country and we hear about it only if a fire or some other catastrophe reveals that the children were left alone.

Separate Lives under One Roof, Then the Great Divide

When parents separate, or begin divorce proceedings and continue living under one roof, serious problems may arise stemming from anger, frustration, guilt, and loss. Add to this the subject of sole or joint custody and even couples who are making the best of a difficult situation can become outright hostile and aggressive. These actions are something children witness, soak up, and react to with behavior I've already outlined.

Parents living in the same house during separation give children false hope because they are saying one thing—that it's all over—but acting as if nothing has changed. That Dad sleeps on the sofa while Mom sleeps in the bedroom would be a cue to children that life isn't exactly like it used to be, but it may not be enough to make them understand how much life is really changing.

Keeping everyone under the same roof may lead to children being let down again. If Mom and Dad say they are getting divorced but then coast along for months living in the same house, their actions don't appear to children like parents getting divorced. For children, divorce starts the minute their parents separate. False hope is probably the most important consideration here. Imagine how devastating it can be for children if they develop a sense that their parents will change their minds and stay together and then, as you and your spouse pass through the various stages of divorce, they start hearing you talk about custody and whom they are going to live with!

As you move to that point, consider what your children are witnessing. They may hear you and your spouse calling each other names or see you throwing things at one another. Even if a relationship has not deteriorated to that level, children see the coldness between you. Once again, they learn what they live, and a cold war going on in the household can be very disconcerting to children.

Despite all that they witness, when asked, children will usually say that they would rather have their parents living in the same house. Frankly, life is easier when both parents are living in the same house.

When custody and placement become issues, life becomes even more difficult for children. They have to start following schedules, trying to keep track of which parent they are to be with on which day. They walk around mumbling, "Well, today is Thursday so I have to pack my suitcase to sleep at Mom's tonight." Calendars—some color-coded for younger children—have to be put on walls at home. Children look at them and read, "Yellow I'm at Mom's, blue is at Dad's and if both colors are on the same day, then I have to share the day with both of them." I've had children look at me in utter confusion, throw their arms in the air, and say, "I can't figure this out. I don't know where I'm supposed to be. Does Wednesday mean Mom's house or Dad's house?"

Under these circumstances, parents need to do all the things they did at the outset of the divorce:

- Don't argue in front of your children.
- Don't pull children into the middle of the custody and placement issue by discussing it in front of them or asking their opinions.
- Don't be abusive to each other in front of your children, and don't think you can get away with calling each other

names and throwing things at each other while they are in their rooms supposedly asleep. They are most suspicious at that time because they expect these emotional explosions to occur when they are thought to be out of earshot.

- Communicate as effectively as you can with one another and with your children.

- Directly saying, "We're still getting divorced even though we're living together" is like putting salt in your children's wounds. Deal with it indirectly, occasionally saying things like, "When your dad and I get divorced . . ." or "In a couple of months when your dad moves out . . ." This reminds children that this is a process.

- Gradually introduce your children to the concept that their living situation may also be changing, but that they should not worry because you will both continue to be active parts of their lives. You might explain: "When Dad and I get divorced, we might have to move to a new, smaller house (or apartment), but we'll make it wonderful together, and you'll be able to see Dad at his new place."

Giving Up Placement

As much as you want custody and placement to be worked out calmly and to the satisfaction of both of you and your children, you must proceed with these issues carefully and with good counsel. Do not act in haste or make such serious decisions under duress or while in the throes of emotional upheaval.

One classic mistake that a parent often makes at the time of separation or divorce is to say to the other, "You take the kids. I need time to adjust" or "I need time to finish school" or to reason, "You have the house and a better income, so you should take the children. When I adjust more (or finish school or have a more substantial living environment), I'll take them back."

Do not give up placement of your children on a temporary basis unless you understand and accept that you may never regain placement of them. It is not unusual, once the interim period has

47

passed, for a parent to request the children's return, only to have the placement parent say, "No way."

Courts generally favor leaving children where they are if life is going smoothly. Therefore, the burden is on the nonplacement parent who wants the children back to prove they would be damaged by remaining where they are. You can't simply argue that you are offering a better environment for them, and that's why you want them back. The other parent generally doesn't have to prove anything.

Grandparents: Help or Hindrance

Grandparents can be invaluable in helping to resolve or mediate such critical decisions as custody and placement. They often see their grandchildren's position more clearly than do parents who are in the heat of the divorce and custody processes, and grandparents are frequently more sensitive and sympathetic to the way divorce affects children. Be aware, however, that grandparents can operate on two different levels.

I have had meetings in which I was trying to mediate with spouses and they just were not making any headway, so I would have them bring their respective sets of parents to the next meeting. Once I had the parents and grandparents in my office, I would tattle on the kids (the parents). I would say, "I just want you to know what's going on here. There's a tremendous amount of immaturity in these two people. They seem to think that fighting is more important than what's good for their child." Then I would look at the grandparents and say, "I need your help. You have a common grandchild here who is being destroyed by what his (her) parents are doing."

Grandparents who are willing to help in this way can be a marvelous resource. Whether we want to admit it or not, no matter how old we get we still want to please our parents. Putting parents into a situation where they must deal with their own parents can change the tone and outcome of mediation.

The other side is that grandparents can have a tremendous negative effect by causing more polarization than is necessary.

48

Because they are parents, they assume a protective position, saying things to their son or daughter such as, "You mean you're going to let that guy who had an affair on you have the kids?" or "How can you forgive her for being drunk all year?" So, we might have a parent trying to do what's best for his or her child, hoping to make custody and placement as easy as possible, but the grandparents are saying, "Don't let that slimeball near the kids."

Although you may want to be as amenable as possible with your former spouse for the good of the children as well as for your own peace of mind, you may find yourself being swayed by your own parents because you are beholden to them. Divorcing couples often turn to their parents for help with the financial burden of divorce (usually in the form of a loan) and sometimes with the upkeep of the children. Grandparents often think that because they are footing the bill, they have the right to have input into decisions. What we end up with, for example, is a dad who knows what's best for his children, but he has just gotten money from his father, who is saying, "Use this money wisely and make sure your wife doesn't get the kids." Dad finds himself in a true conflict position.

Every state in the union allows for grandparents to have visitation rights with their grandchildren. If you oppose grandparents' visitation, you are likely to lose that battle in court unless you can demonstrate that the children would be damaged or in danger by spending time with their grandparents.

The standard is to allow grandparents one visitation a month. This could be a daytime or overnight visit. The most frequent problems arise when children are residing with one parent and the parents of the former spouse want to visit. Just because your ex-spouse was someone you could not get along with does not necessarily mean his or her parents are an equal problem.

A difficult situation that may arise during grandparents' visitation is if the grandparents lobby for their child by saying negative things about the other parent. Statements like, "Your mother doesn't . . ." or "Your father isn't . . ." are not helpful for anyone, but can be destructive. If grandparents end up being very destructive, they may lose the right to have contact with their grandchildren.

The custody and placement process is an exercise in balancing difficult choices and players, much like all other parts of the divorce process. Now that you have an understanding of custody and placement options, you probably have some ideas about what is right for your situation. Ideally, you and your spouse will be in agreement about what would work best for both of you and your children. However, such agreement is often not the case. In either event, you will need to work out the arrangements through the courts.

▼
Chapter

4

Navigating the Legal Waters

People caught in the heat of divorce and custody issues may look upon the legal process as nothing more than a quagmire, fraught with dangers waiting to suck them under. Some men and women allow themselves to become so overwhelmed by their emotions and by the enormous financial and child-rearing responsibilities that are thrust on them during this period that they can't see the proverbial forest from the trees. That's when they know it's time to seek the advice and security of an attorney.

Finding an Attorney

This can be one of the costliest moves you'll ever make in your life, but in some cases if you don't have a good attorney, the intangible and tangible costs to you and your children may be higher than you ever imagined. Attorneys' fees can be high, especially if you are embroiled in a drawn-out custody dispute. There are alternatives to litigation, however, including arbitration and mediation. As far as I'm concerned, mediation is one of the potential bright lights in this process and one very viable possibility for parents.

In mediation, parents try to work out agreements on divorce and custody issues with the help of an impartial, objective third party (mediator), who never tells them what to do, but who can make suggestions and try to keep the process moving forward. In arbitration, the third party (arbitrator) listens to you and your spouse, then he or she decides what you will do. Each of these approaches has pros and cons, which I will talk about later. With these approaches, an attorney can be your objective third party and offer you the benefit of his or her experience without the high cost of litigation.

Most people choose to have legal counsel represent them in divorce cases, particularly if child custody is an issue. Selecting an attorney in a divorce case is a much more important task than most people realize. Unfortunately, many people are willing to choose attorneys based on cost or whether they know the attorney from a previous setting, or for other less important reasons.

People often choose an attorney for a divorce action based on what happened in cases involving their friends or relatives. This information can be helpful. However, each case is different, and it can be difficult to generalize about how well someone represented an individual without knowing all the facts firsthand. You may think you know them, but your knowledge of what actually happened will be filtered through your friend's or relative's perceptions.

All too often, the results achieved in a case hinge on the competency of the attorney, and not the merits of the case itself. Competency is obviously an important issue. However, even the most competent attorney cannot pull rabbits out of hats. The implication here is that, all things being equal, the more competent the attorney is, the more likely he or she is to get better results for clients.

You must ask several questions when considering hiring an attorney based on someone else's experience:

- Did the attorney identify all the issues?
- Was the divorce amicable?
- Was the attorney who represented your friend's spouse equal to, better than, or less competent than the one who represented your friend?

Recommendations from friends and family members can also be problematic because someone might think his or her attorney achieved good results when, in fact, the outcome could have been much better. Others may think the results were terrible, but their expectations may have been unrealistically high, and no one could have gotten what they wanted. Talking to a friend or relative may be helpful, but remember, their opinions are only one factor that should be considered.

Other factors should be kept in mind when choosing an attorney. First of all, remember that it is better to mediate or negotiate a divorce settlement than to go to court and fight it out. Consequently, your attorney should have strong negotiating skills. Although the barracuda approach might work well on television, it's usually best to keep the sharks out of the water when children are involved. However, if your spouse won't agree to mediate or mediation breaks down, you will need a lawyer with good courtroom skills.

In addition to good negotiation and courtroom skills, it is critical that your lawyer be experienced in divorce and custody cases. Another mistake people often make is hiring the attorney who handled their house closing, represented them in a minor automobile accident case, or negotiated their office lease. These generalist attorneys may not have the family law sophistication necessary to successfully represent your case. Family law is very complex and you have a lot at stake. You need an experienced family lawyer to lead you through this terrain. Look for an attorney who devotes at least half of his or her practice to family law.

Don't try to cut corners by hiring a friend or family member who happens to be a lawyer. If he or she knows both parents, the lawyer is put into the difficult position of having to take sides. In addition, people tend not to listen to the advice of their attorney friends as much as they would if a nonfriend attorney was representing them. In the end, this shortcut could not only hurt your case, but also cost you a friendship.

Finally, don't be penny-wise and pound-foolish when selecting an attorney. Most family lawyers charge by the hour. I have seen a large number of cases in which individuals picked the lawyer with the cheapest rates and did not end up with the best results, particularly when their spouses had used more appropriate criteria in choosing an attorney.

Selecting an attorney based on his or her initial cost estimate may not save you the money you think it will. An inexperienced attorney with a lower hourly rate may take many more hours than an experienced attorney who can cut to the basic issues quickly and efficiently. You may also end up spending more money if a less-experienced attorney fails to initially address all the necessary issues in your case and you have to return to court.

To pick the attorney who is right for you, talk to friends who have been divorced and have been pleased with their representation, keeping in mind issues discussed in this chapter. Once you have a list of potential attorneys, narrow it down by meeting with them to determine the lawyer that you are most comfortable with and that you believe will best represent your interests. Many attorneys will not charge for an initial consultation of up to one hour and some charge a nominal fee for the first meeting, but ask about that when you make the appointment.

You can also check the Yellow Pages for family law attorneys. However, you must remember that advertising may not completely represent what an attorney is capable of doing.

Many other resources are available when you're looking for an attorney. A book called the *Martindale-Hubbell Law Directory* can be found in the reference sections of many large public libraries as well as in law libraries. This book lists attorneys by specialization, locale, and qualifications. *The Best Lawyers in America* is another good reference book. An attorney cannot buy his or her way into this book. Before a name is listed in this book, the attorney's background is investigated and he or she is included only if found to be highly qualified.

Local bar associations can also be helpful because they will provide names of attorneys according to specialization. This resource is valuable, however, only if the association requires members to be credentialed in some way. In some cases, an attorney need only submit his or her name to be included on a bar association list. Don't hesitate to ask what the association's criteria is for membership. Various states also have academies of family lawyers, whose members have undergone some form of screening for inclusion in the organization. Other professionals, such as accountants, therapists, and other lawyers, can also provide good referrals. Be willing to reach out to people you know and can trust.

Don't Be Attracted by Unrealistic Promises

From the outset, be wary of any attorney who makes unrealistic promises or guarantees that he or she will get you everything you want. Attorneys who say they will definitely get you custody of your children, who promise to "nail your spouse to the wall," or who lay out a plan that includes bringing experts into the case who they know will testify on your behalf may be promising things they cannot deliver. You should be especially concerned if an attorney is promising things you previously lost in other court hearings or trials, or that other attorneys have indicated are not possible. A more realistic attorney will offer a good likelihood that he or she will be able to prevail on certain issues, but will offer no guarantee. You are in a vulnerable period of your life when you are getting divorced and seeking custody. Because of your heightened emotional state, you should be extra cautious about the people with whom you choose to work.

Your attorney has an obligation to be realistic and not hold out false hope. Based on knowledge of the legal system, an attorney should tell you what you need to hear, not what you want to hear. You want someone who will represent you fully and present all arguments on your behalf outside the office, but who, in the office behind closed doors, will be completely honest with you about your chances.

Asking a potential attorney these questions during the initial meeting should help you make an informed and educated decision:

- What are your hourly and day rates?
- Can you give me an estimate of what the entire case will cost, including any custody dispute?
- How much of your work is spent dealing with divorces and custody issues? Do you consider this your area of expertise? What other kinds of law do you practice? (As I said earlier, you don't want your divorce and custody issues handled by someone who spends most of the time on house closings.)
- Are mediation or arbitration options in my case? Would you be comfortable operating in these settings on my behalf?
- Realistically, what are my chances of achieving what I want in this case? What are my chances of getting custody of my children? What are my options?
- How long do you think this case will run?
- Will you be available when I need you to represent me? (You do not want an attorney so overburdened that your case is handled "when he or she gets around to it," thereby creating postponements and delays.)

Avoid "Hired Guns" and "Dirty Tricks" Attorneys

Any time an attorney suggests actions that give you a sense of dirty tricks, a giant red flag should go up. Every community has its share of attorneys who are known for using dirty tricks in divorce cases. Although these lawyers may sound clever and promising and as if they are on your side, these attorneys are well-known by judges and often do not get the results in court that they have promised.

Dirty tricks attorneys who encourage you to participate in their schemes can lead you into a situation that will surely backfire. Once you start participating in these tricks, your children will become involved in the plotting and manipulating, which is something you want to avoid.

Children can't help getting involved in this behavior because it happens around them and they are sensitive to it, especially if they're young. Teenagers are apt to say, "You can play your silly games but leave me out of it." It's too risky for younger children to say something like that because such comments can lead to disciplinary action from the parent. Often, youngsters don't even recognize the motivation behind the actions of the parent and the dirty tricks lawyer.

On the same continuum with manipulation is lying, which can set children up for disappointment. Children who are enlisted into participating in dirty tricks may be led to expect some outcome in their favor. If the tricks fail, children are let down. From moral and ethical viewpoints, dirty tricks give children the wrong message.

Be forewarned that dirty tricks lawyers don't just play these tricks on the other side—they also play them on their clients. For example, two lawyers may have lunch to discuss a case and they spend about ten minutes during their meal talking about it. At the end of the lunch, the dirty tricks lawyer will say: "Just so our records are comparable, I'm going to bill my client for a two-hour conference with you." The other lawyer, if reputable, will say that he or she is only billing for the ten minutes. The rationale here is simple: A person who uses that kind of mentality in one aspect of the practice is going to use it in all aspects of the practice.

Parents involved in dirty tricks cases, have told me that they were afraid I would not recognize the manipulation on the part of their husbands or wives. And that is the most difficult thing for me to do as an evaluator because some people are artful manipulators. Let me illustrate how this can create more upheaval in a divorce case than might otherwise be expected. I recall a case in which the judge made an order nobody liked. The mother wanted to move to Arizona and was pleading her case that her daughter should move with her. After two and a half days of testimony, the judge became angry and said, "I don't want to listen to this anymore. I want to settle this case. Your daughter goes to Arizona with her mother for fifth grade, comes back to Milwaukee with her father for the sixth grade, goes back to Mom for the seventh grade, and returns to Dad for the eighth grade. Then we'll decide where she goes to high school for four years."

After that happened, the mother's attorney told me on the phone, "This case needs dirty tricks and that's why I brought another attorney into it." He was referring to someone who specialized in dirty tricks. The dirty tricks attorney came into the case and did such things as take the child's court-appointed guardian on a trip to Arizona. When the court heard about this, the child was ordered back into her father's custody, whether that was the most appropriate place for her to be or not. The dirty tricks backfired and really upset the judge.

Utilization of a dirty tricks attorney can be compounded by using a hired gun expert. All communities have experts with reputations for testifying in the direction of the person who hires them. Hired guns are people who are described as authorities in various fields or professions and who are brought into cases as expert witnesses. As is true of the attorneys, the courts know who these people are and their testimony tends to carry less weight than the testimony of experts who are considered truly independent.

Reputable lawyers also know who the dirty tricks attorneys and hired gun experts are. If you approach a reputable lawyer after having used a dirty tricks lawyer or hired gun expert, he or she will probably tell you that overcoming the problems associated with having used such an individual will be more expensive than if you had used a reputable attorney from the outset.

Switching Attorneys

As the old adage says, don't switch horses in midstream. This advice also applies to switching attorneys. Once you have hired an attorney, try to stick with him or her. Using a series of attorneys over time may present problems in a divorce case. It is not in any way unreasonable for someone to not mesh well with an attorney, necessitating finding a new one. However, if you are into your fourth, fifth, or sixth attorney, people are going to ask why. You may feel you have legitimate reasons for switching that many times. However, the courts and other individuals involved in the process are going to wonder what prompted so many changes. If you find yourself often wanting to switch because of the advice attorneys are giving you, it may be that you are having difficulty accepting their advice, even though the advice may be reasonable and accurate for your case. If you are looking for someone to tell you what you want to hear, as opposed to what is realistic, and switch often enough, you are likely to eventually find an attorney who will support your position even if it may be unlikely that he or she will be able to deliver what you want.

When you switch attorneys, you are apt to incur additional expenses because the new attorney must take the time to become familiar with your case. Also, his or her predecessors may have done things that were not the best alternatives, but the new attorney is stuck with them and will need extra time to work out the best course of action to take under those circumstances.

It can be disconcerting to see your attorney interacting in a friendly manner in a courtroom or the halls of a courthouse with your spouse's attorney, especially when you may feel that you are at war with your spouse. It can be equally upsetting to see the attorneys make plans to go to lunch with one another or play golf after they have represented you in a bitterly contested case. Attorneys can be friendly with one another and still represent you fairly and fully. Since attorneys are bound by a professional code of ethics, you have a right to expect yours to represent you in a professional capacity.

Telling Your Story

If your custody dispute ends up being tried in court, you will probably be required to testify. Direct examination is when your attorney questions you. You can expect him or her to spend a considerable amount of time preparing you for direct examination. It is more difficult, however, for your attorney to prepare you for questions that will be asked by your spouse's attorney, called cross-examination.

Cross-examination is typically a more uncomfortable experience than direct examination. Be as relaxed as possible and, as the oath requires, tell the truth. Remember that it is your spouse's attorney's job to ask you difficult questions to support his or her client's position. This does not mean your spouse's attorney dislikes or hates you or is out to get you.

Acting as Your Own Attorney

An alternative to hiring an attorney is to represent yourself, which is called pro se (pronounced "pro say"). For people who can successfully negotiate placement and financial arrangements with their spouse, pro se is a wonderful approach. There is no reason why you should spend large sums of money for attorneys if you can adequately represent yourselves. Many communities have divorce pro se organizations that help people with the paperwork of divorce, explain the practicalities of the legal process, and offer advice for a relatively nominal fee.

Pro se, however, is not always the best approach to use. If your spouse has hired an attorney, you will be at a major disadvantage if you go pro se. Imagine being in a courtroom and representing yourself pro se when the attorney on the other side objects to a question citing specific legal cases to support the objection. You are not going to be in a position to adequately respond to those objections. Even if money is an obstacle, you owe it to yourself and your children to seek an equitable settlement. Don't go the pro se route unless your spouse agrees to do the same.

Mediation as a First Step

Whether or not you hire any attorney, mediation is a good first step toward trying to reach a fair settlement. The best quote I have heard about why mediation should be used is "It is better to send your children to college than your attorney's children."

Many states require mediation before an individual is allowed to litigate a custody case, and mediation has become popular even

60

where it is not required by law. If you choose to use mediation, you must select an individual who has appropriate credentials in this area. Many people call themselves mediators, but have no specific training for it. The Academy of Family Mediators is an organization that accredits mediators. A divorce can be either fully or partially mediated, meaning certain issues are resolved in mediation while others must be settled in court if you cannot agree on them. Issues that can be resolved in mediation include custody and placement, financial terms, and division of property. Ordinarily, one person would mediate the divorce in a neutral capacity, although sometimes two mediators are used, one to represent the interests of each parent.

Mediation carries a number of advantages. The divorce can be resolved quickly and inexpensively. The mediation process generally costs a fraction of what litigation costs. It also leaves fewer scars on family members compared to going through the adversarial or litigation approach. Mediated cases are much less likely to be taken back to court than cases that were initially litigated. The mediation process takes into account each party's wishes and desires and tries to fashion a compromise solution. As I mentioned before, the mediator does not tell you what you should do or how you should do it. Instead, he or she tries to broker an arrangement acceptable to both parties. If you or your spouse are not happy with the final solution, you can simply walk away.

Choosing mediation does not mean that you cannot use an attorney. When I perform a mediation, I encourage the parties to take the mediated agreement to their respective attorneys to put it into legal language and draw up a stipulation that the parties can then sign and enter with their divorce decree. If an attorney objects to some of the language in the agreement, the parties can go back to mediation and rework some of the issues. This also holds true down the road if new issues arise.

Just as parents should not deal with the financial arrangements of a divorce in front of the children, likewise they should not discuss the process of getting a lawyer or what transpires in mediation in front of them. One problem created by allowing children to hear about these processes is that the parent is usually at such a high level of anxiety that it's difficult for the children to not be affected by that stress. Such discussions may indicate to the children (if they don't already know it) that the divorce process is going to be filled with anxiety and that they had better get ready for a rough ride. They may also hear Mom, for example, saying, "I've got to get the best attorney to fight for us." Children then get the additional message that a fight is likely to occur. A related point to consider is that children who see parents agonizing over their representation are given the impression that too much of the power over what is going to happen to them will fall to an attorney instead of their parents.

One of the biggest advantages of mediation is that it gets the parents talking and puts them in a position where they must try to deal with each other in a reasonable way. This is crucial learning time for when they have to work with each other in the future about matters concerning their children, especially if they have been at each other's throat for a long time. I'm not talking about lip service mediation, meaning that you go once and the mediator writes a letter to the court saying this occurred, but that you've really had no meaningful dialogue or positive outcome. I'm talking about meaningful, hands-on, ongoing mediation, in which parents become aware of a more comfortable way to approach issues.

Mediation sets a very positive example for children, especially if they have seen you arguing a lot. Now they see you talking to each other and to them about what the ultimate plan is going to be, and children think maybe this isn't going to be as bad as they thought.

Mediation also indirectly affects children because good mediation costs about one tenth of what good lawyering costs. Parents, instead of spending an enormous amount of money going to trial, may spend $1,000 mediating a case, and they undergo less frustration and arguing and put less financial strain on the family.

The only negative that I see to mediation is when the process breaks down after children have been given hope. Some mediation cases break down because parents cannot come to terms with one another.

The mediation and arbitration approaches have many advantages. I've already said that mediation is less expensive, both psychologically and financially. Perhaps the most important advantage of mediation, however, is that you participate in decisions affecting you and your children instead of deferring to a stranger—a judge. Even if a judge is the best in the world, you run the risk of him or her reaching a decision that is different from what you or your spouse wants.

Although mediation is certainly a preferable approach to resolving problems, individuals can in no way mediate an agreement for a four-year-old child, for example, that is going to work for the next 14 years. Relationships change, children grow, school placements change, medical issues arise, and many other factors come into play between childhood and legal age adulthood. You must understand the likelihood that the initial mediation agreement will need modification as children get older. In most cases, when mediation is working well, parents can reach a modified agreement on their own. However, if mediation worked the first time, you should not be reluctant to go back and re-mediate the agreement when circumstances change.

I cannot emphasize enough how important it is to consider mediation to resolve differences in custody cases. Even if a mediated agreement requires difficult compromises, you and your children are spared the powerful negative effects of a court battle. Remember that if mediation does not work, litigation is always available to you. Hence, nothing is lost by first attempting mediation.

Arbitration

Arbitration offers another way of reaching an agreement without going to court. Abitration exists in many forms, and it can be binding or nonbinding. Binding arbitration requires the parties to accept the arbitrator's recommendation. Nonbinding arbitration allows individuals to disagree with the arbitrator and attempt to find another solution. Unfortunately, nonbinding arbitration often has little effect because either party can disagree with the result and start the process over again.

Retired judges are often used as arbitrators. They have expertise in dispute resolution and have learned from years on the bench how to resolve problems. However, it is not unusual for attorneys and/or psychologists to serve as arbitrators in divorce cases.

Mediation and arbitration can be used in combination with one another. Arbitration can be an effective tool when the mediation process breaks down and leaves a number of minor issues to be resolved that don't require going to court. This process generally involves each of you telling your side of the story or stating your position and the arbitrator making a decision that supports one side or the other or is somewhere in the middle.

I know of a case, for example, in which the two principals, Mary and Jim, had mediated all aspects of their divorce. They were down to the last thousand dollars worth of personal property, which included a list of items several pages long. None of the items was worth more than $75. It was apparent that Jim and Mary were more interested in arguing with one another at that point than in reaching a resolution. The mediator scheduled three more sessions and said if they could not reach agreement after that, he would then serve as an arbitrator and divide the items. It was not too surprising that Mary and Jim were able to reach an agreement before those three sessions were up. If this combination approach is used, it is necessary for both parties to sign an agreement in advance that they understand the process and will not back out after the mediator/arbitrator has made a decision.

The Court Process

Temporary Orders

Whether you are mediating an agreement or litigating a case, at some time early in the process you will go to court either representing yourself or with an attorney to get temporary orders pertaining to placement of your children. Temporary orders are often issued by someone other than the judge who will hear your case. These individuals have such titles as "marital master" or "family court commissioner."

Don't be fooled by the term *temporary orders*. Although these orders are intended to address placement, placement schedules, and support only for the period between the temporary order and the divorce, judges tend to resist change. Consequently, the parent who receives placement of a child through temporary orders will have an advantage when the case goes to court. Even though you can have it written into the temporary orders that they were made "without prejudice" to any of the parties, judges are still reluctant to make a change when it is not necessary.

The phrase *without prejudice* written into a temporary order suggests that when the trial occurs, these issues will be readdressed in court. Again, however, if children are placed with one parent as a result of temporary orders and life seems to be going well, a judge is not likely to upset the apple cart and require the children to change placement without knowing how they would react to another environment.

The period of time that temporary orders are in effect often serves as a trial period to see how things will go. If during this time the parent with placement exercises poor judgment, if problems arise in school or at home, if contact with the other parent is obstructed, or if similar problems arise, these factors will be held against that parent at the trial and may lead to a reversal of placement.

You need temporary orders because if the relationship between you and your former spouse is acrimonious enough for you to divorce, a custody dispute is likely to occur. You are not going to be angry enough with each other to dissolve your marriage and then say, "Let's sit down and work out a placement arrangement that's best for the kids." Temporary orders allow someone with a level head to review your case and make a decision about where the children will stay, at least temporarily. These orders also help prevent parents from interfering with visitation. If you are displeased with temporary orders, you can request a review by a judge.

Children love to press their ears to doors to hear everything that is being discussed or argued about by their parents. Even if you are trying to keep them out of these discussions, children are apt to have an indication of what's being planned. One of the negatives of temporary orders is that they stretch out children's anxiety over how long a living arrangement will last, and children worry anew about where they are going to live and with whom. When you hear a child ask, "Where am I going to live?" you can understand how emotional this can be.

If your children are concerned about temporary placement, try to soothe and reassure them, but don't give them false hope or a message that's untrue because, as I said, the orders may become permanent. Instead of telling children that placement is temporary, you might say, "There are a lot of things happening now that might not be the way we'd like them to be. If we go to court, the judge will tell us the way it's going to be, but right now we'll just do the best we can."

Children can become very dramatic when a temporary order changes to a different permanent order that runs counter to what they want. A child may threaten to run away or even to kill himself or herself. Odds very strongly favor a child doing neither, but in some cases they do carry out their threats.

How do you know when children are being genuine about threats? It is sometimes difficult for parents to know, so I encourage them to get children into therapy as soon as even one such threat is made. Children who do run away can turn to organizations such as Pathfinders in Milwaukee, Wis. (many cities have organizations like this), for a safe haven and therapeutic care until they can go back home or are placed elsewhere.

One safeguard that can be taken if a child threatens to run away rather than live with a particular parent is to go to court and tell the judge that a placement recommendation is counter to what the child wants and that he or she has threatened to run away. Before the child learns that the placement order has been put into effect, the courts and mental health professionals have a chance to set up a safety net and get the child into therapy.

You don't have time to set up such an arrangement in a situation where a child has already been placed and says, "If you make me continue living with Dad (Mom) I'll kill myself." A child who is making a statement about where he or she IS, not where he or she doesn't want to be is raising a red flag. Parents facing this should immediately ask the courts, their attorneys, court-appointed guardians, and psychologists to take action, which can include putting a child into psychiatric placement, changing placement, and therapy. One reason children make such statements is because they are impulsive by nature and don't think through the alternatives. Therapeutic intervention gives them an opportunity to consider all the options.

Custody Disputes

If you discover that custody issues aren't resolvable through a non-litigation process, the first thing you should do is put a support network in place. Make sure you have appropriate legal representation. Tell family and friends that you are involved in a custody dispute and that you are likely to need to lean on them for additional support. If you are a religious person, turn to clergy. It may also be the time for you to consider meeting with a therapist or counselor to make sure your approach to decision making is as objective as possible and in your children's best interests. Whereas friends, relatives, and clergy are likely to blindly support you, serving as advocate supporters and not as objective supporters, a therapist or counselor will provide objectivity, ensuring that you look at issues from many different viewpoints.

Many people choose to avoid custody disputes out of concern for the negative effects they will have on them and/or their children. Sometimes, however, custody disputes are unavoidable. The following information can help you understand what is likely to happen in a custody dispute.

The Guardian Ad Litem

A guardian ad litem is appointed by the court to represent the best interests of the children. In most states, guardians ad litem are attorneys; however, courts in some states appoint nonattorneys as guardians ad litem.

In my experience, two types of attorneys become guardians ad litem. The first is the novice attorney, a recent law school graduate who looks at guardian ad litem appointments as a means of obtaining work and becoming known in the family law community. These individuals may not be adequately trained for guardian ad litem work or fully understand what is necessary to sufficiently fulfill the role of guardian ad litem. Many states require specialized training for attorneys before they can become guardians ad litem; however, some states require no training or only pay cursory attention to training.

The second type of person who becomes a guardian ad litem is the attorney who is truly devoted to understanding the needs of children and considers this a major part of his or her practice. These attorneys have been involved in family law for many years, in some instances decades, and they understand child development and are capable of communicating well with children. They also see objectively the needs of parents and children, and make recommendations that match their needs.

The two best guardians ad litem I have worked with were middle school teachers prior to becoming lawyers. By virtue of their teaching backgrounds, both had experience with children and understood their developmental needs.

Many experienced lawyers won't take guardian ad litem assigments because sometimes it's ugly work, and in some jurisdictions they have to accept the court's pay rate, which can be as low as $35 per hour. In cases involving parents who are financially secure, the courts appoint experienced attorneys to do guardian ad litem work and order that they be paid at their regular rate.

At the beginning of this process, parents usually don't know if a guardian ad litem will be appointed. However, if one is appointed, children literally get their own attorney. Children have probably heard their parents talk about their attorneys and may have a jaded perception of what an attorney will or will not do for them. If parents have given the impression that attorneys fight for their clients, a child may think the guardian ad litem is a person who is going to fight for him or her, which may reduce a child's anxiety. On the other hand, if a parent has made negative comments about the other parent's attorney, a child may initially have little trust in the guardian ad litem.

Children have no way of gauging a guardian ad litem's competency, but they recognize if someone is caring and understanding and makes them feel comfortable and less anxious. Children tend to connect with a guardian ad litem who knows how to communicate with them and understands their needs. In some cases, however, children are saddled with guardians ad litem who are literally afraid to talk to the children because they don't know how. Children never connect with those people.

In very, very few cases is a guardian ad litem appointed at the beginning. A situation has to become extremely messy and ugly for this to be done. Even in cases that aren't that bad, however, many children see a considerable amount of ugliness as their parents move through the divorce and custody processes. In most cases, when a guardian ad litem is introduced, he or she is expected to raise a child's comfort level, and it may be very difficult for a child to respond positively because for so long nobody has been looking out for his or her interests.

I was involved in one case in which the guardian ad litem for an eight-year-old girl named Michelle was not very good. Michelle needed a strong, competent, understanding guardian ad litem because she was at the center of an extremely difficult custody dispute.

Michelle's mother had involved her in many of the things from which children should be excluded, such as manipulation and lying. For example, Michelle left a message for me one holiday at 10:35 P.M. on my office voice mail. She said hello and there followed a series of ums and uhs. I could hear her mother whispering in the background, but Michelle said nothing except ums for the entire length of the two-and-a-half-minute message. The next message was also from Michelle. She started out with ums and uhs, but then said, "I just wanted to tell you that I want to live with my mom. I don't like it with my dad." Then she hung up.

Her mother had become so desperate to gain placement of Michelle that she put this incredible pressure on the child by making her call on a holiday, past her bedtime, to deliver what appeared to be her mother's message. Courts, upon hearing about such behavior, are very reluctant to place a child with that parent. Such a parent is undermining his or her own efforts without realizing it.

Michelle trusted and loved both her parents, and she was not going to choose one over the other. She was being pushed into that position by her mother, who moved 30 miles away from her ex-spouse as part of her manipulation. Her argument for wanting custody was that she lived far away and it was difficult for her to visit Michelle because of the distance.

Michelle's mother convinced the child, who was living with her father, that she was going to be allowed to live with her mother. She told Michelle not to sign up for any activities at school because she would have to leave them when she went to a new school. Michelle's interpretation was that she didn't have to do homework, and asked, "Why do I have to work in this school when I'm going to end up in another school soon?"

Michelle ended up living with her father, after having gone through a year of school without accomplishing much. Because her mother had assured Michelle of living with her, Michelle was very disappointed when the decision favored her father. We started seeing the depression, regression, or acting out behavior that I talked about earlier in this book.

Michelle's mother poisoned the child against the guardian ad litem because he made temporary recommendations that were counter to her plan. As a result, Michelle would tell me that the guardian ad litem had lied to me, or that "I don't like him because he made me live with Dad and go to Dad's school." She was actually attending the same school she had attended before her parents divorced, which was the correct recommendation from the guardian ad litem. Because Michelle's mother didn't speak too highly of the guardian ad litem, who was Michelle going to believe and trust: A virtual stranger, who her mother said was bad, or her mom, who was making all sorts of promises to her? Michelle did not have a good relationshp with her guardian ad litem, which was unfortunate because had he been more experienced and had her mother not talked about him so badly, he may have been able to help Michelle balance the confusion she felt about her situation and help keep her mother slightly more under control.

In the case of the four children that we discussed in Chapter 3, the guardian ad litem came into the picture four years after the case began. She was the second guardian ad litem in that case, because it had been closed and the first guardian ad litem dismissed. (Usually a guardian ad litem is dismissed after a trial or within six months after a trial. If a guardian ad litem is needed after that, sometimes a new one is appointed.)

In this case, a second guardian ad litem was appointed because the mother wanted to move to Florida, a considerable distance from where she and her children and her ex-spouse were living. This would have interfered with the father's visitation time. The guardian ad litem was called in to see if the move was necessary. These children were already having a difficult time when along came this stranger saying, "Trust me. I'm going to act in your best interests." These children had been through so much that they had no idea who to trust. But they were fortunate to get a very competent, caring guardian ad litem who earned their trust. They warmed up to her and started calling her by her first name. When crises arose, she came to my office to meet with the children and we talked to them together. It was easy to see the warm, trusting interaction between them, but that was based on the guardian ad litem's behavior, not on the children.

The mother in that case also tried to turn the children against the guardian ad litem. However, because the guardian ad litem was active with the children and they could see what she was doing for them, their mother was not successful. In Michelle's case, the poisoning worked because the guardian ad litem was not as involved.

The Custody Study

A guardian ad litem appointed in a case often recommends that a custody study be performed. This study may be done by a county-paid social worker who interviews the parents, makes home visits, and makes collateral contacts in the community before making a recommendation. Since the guardian ad litem and the person conducting the custody study are both court-appointed and are most likely paid by the court, the court will listen closely to their recommendations. Therefore, do not underestimate the importance of the input from the custody study and the guardian ad litem. When these people call to make an appointment as part of the divorce process, take their roles seriously, make yourself available, and be honest.

Custody Evaluation

A custody evaluation generally involves formalized testing along with interviews, contact with collateral sources, and meetings with attorneys. Custody evaluations are most frequently performed by doctoral-level psychologists with specialized training and experience in developmental psychology, family psychology, psychological assessment of adults and children, psychopathology of adults and children, the effects of divorce and custody arrangements on adults and children, relevant aspects of the legal system, research, theory, policy, and practice regarding divorce and child custody issues, and a working knowledge of the Ethical Principles and Code of Conduct for Psychologists.

A typical custody evaluation entails 4 to 10 hours of testing and interviewing per person, at an average cost of $500 to $1,000 per person. A psychologist is called into a case to perform a custody evaluation when the court, guardian ad litem, and/or either of the parent's attorneys feels that a person's mental health may adversely affect the children.

The American Psychological Association has developed guidelines for custody evaluations. As an informed consumer (whenever you hire a professional, you are acting as a consumer), you should know what to expect from the evaluation and the psychologist, and what the outcome is likely to be.

The main purpose of a custody evaluation is to determine what is in the best psychological interests of the children. Linking children's interests and well-being, the focus of the evaluation is on parenting capacity, the psychological and developmental needs of the children, and the resulting fit. The goal of the psychologist is not to assess whether the parents have any psychological or emotional problems, but to evaluate how they function on a day-to-day basis in their parental roles.

When you enter a custody evaluation setting, the most important factor to remember is to be honest. Being honest may sometimes appear detrimental to your position, but if a psychologist learns that you were dishonest, it is likely to weigh heavily against you. You can also safely assume that the psychologist will find out about issues you are trying to hide, because in a custody dispute, your spouse is interested in making you look as bad as possible and will gladly share such information with the psychologist.

Psychologists doing custody evaluations usually have access to records of arrests and other problems with the law, Child Protective Services reports, mental health records, and alcohol and other drug abuse records. You can assume that the psychologist will check your rendition of what has occurred against official documents.

The frequency and recent nature of mental health problems and problems with the law are important issues. A parent who has been hospitalized in psychiatric units 10 times in the three years prior to the custody evaluation is much worse off than a parent who had one hospitalization 15 years earlier or as a teenager. Additionally, someone who has been involved in a number of crimes against persons, such as sexual assault, armed robbery, or assault and battery, is looked upon much more negatively than is a person who has been involved in misdemeanor crimes against property.

The psychologist will be interested in observing you with your children as part of the evaluation process. These observations can take place a number of ways and the approach depends on the psychologist's preference. The most effective way is for each parent to be observed alone with each child under six years of age. Another effective way is for the psychologist to see a parent with all the children together to determine how well he or she can handle them as a group.

Don't become too anxious about this observation period. It is likely to be short and rarely will it be the key element upon which a psychologist bases his or her recommendation. As much as possible, be yourself. Be relaxed and as natural as you can be.

Psychologists often feel that a formal observation with children over six years of age is unnecessary. Instead, they might watch the interaction between parents and the children in a waiting room or at other informal times.

A question often raised about observations is whether they should be allowed to occur between children and alleged abuse perpetrators, or between children and a parent when a restraining order is in place. One purpose of the psychological evaluation is to determine if abuse has occurred, if sufficient bonding between child and parent merits continued contacts, and/or if supervised or unsupervised visitation should be recommended.

Attorneys may strongly object to their client's children being in the company of a parent who has been accused of abuse or against whom a restraining order has been issued. However, psychologists have no other way to adequately evaluate interaction between parents and children. Courts recognize that the evaluator is a trained mental health professional who is obligated to act in the best interest of children. As a result, the evaluator will not allow the interaction to become psychologically or physically harmful.

Psychologists are obligated to take an impartial stance in custody evaluations. For this reason, the psychologist should be appointed by the court, the guardian ad litem, or agreed on by both parents' attorneys.

When a psychologist is called on to perform a second opinion evaluation, he or she is still required to remain objective and impartial. Therefore, don't assume that if you hire a psychologist to do a second opinion evaluation, the results will automatically favor you.

As I said earlier, a psychologist must have specialized competence to perform a custody evaluation. When a psychologist is asked to help determine whether sexual abuse has taken place, he or she must address many variables. The behavior of the child should be evaluated to see if it is similar to individuals who have been abused. The alleged perpetrator's behavior should be evaluated to determine if it is similiar to that of sexual abusers. And, the behavior of the nonperpetrating parent should also be evaluated for similarities with behavior of nonperpetrating parents.

74

After all this, however, even the most competent psychologist may not be able to determine with any degree of certainty that abuse has occurred.

When a psychologist performs a custody evaluation, various questions will need to be answered, especially if one parent has made allegations of abuse against the other. These questions could be asked by the court, the guardian ad litem, either or both parents' attorneys, or the parents. Questions might include:

- Was the child sexually abused?
- Was the child physically abused?
- Will it be detrimental to the child to move to a different city?
- Do either of the parents' drug-related problems in the past present a threat to the child?
- Does the mental health of either parent pose a problem or threat to the child?

The psychologist should be made aware of these questions in advance so that the evaluation can be as thorough as possible.

To save money, psychologists are sometimes asked to perform a partial evaluation; that is, they are to evaluate only the parents, only the children, or one parent and the children without the other parent. Partial evaluations may save time and money, but they do not allow a psychologist to render a complete opinion. When a partial evaluation is performed, the psychologist should tell you and your attorney that limitations in his or her recommendations will be necessary. When only one parent is evaluated, the psychologist can state whether the parent is psychologically stable, but cannot make a custody recommendation. Evaluating parents without the children makes it impossible for the evaluator to take children's developmental needs into consideration. Similarly, evaluating children without their parents does not allow a psychologist to consider parenting capabilities.

Informed Consent

It is important to obtain the informed consent of all participants before a psychologist performs a custody evaluation. This means that the psychologist should tell you the nature, purpose, and method of evaluation, who has requested it, and who will pay the fees. In most cases, either the court or the parents pay. When parents cannot afford it, courts may advance the funds and allow them to pay the court back over time. In most cases, courts will find a way of dividing the cost of evaluations between parents, based on ability to pay. However, in cases in which one parent brought the action, the courts may require that parent to bear the full cost.

As I mentioned, as part of the informed consent process, you should be made aware of what will take place during the evaluation. This will generally include a description of the psychological testing, what collateral contacts will be made, what additional documentation might be sought, and how the information will be reported. In most cases, psychologists will also want to meet with the guardian ad litem and/or both attorneys, and you should be told in advance if such a meeting is going to take place.

Clarifying financial arrangements is also part of informed consent. Many psychologists require you to sign a custody evaluation agreement that includes the areas discussed in informed consent and financial arrangements. Most experienced psychologists require the full cost of the evaluation to be paid in the form of a retainer, or at least be paid prior to issuing a report. Some psychologists charge a set fee per evaluation while others have an hourly rate. This must be disclosed in the informed consent.

You should expect no surprises regarding costs. A psychologist is required to identify at the outset any additional services that are not included in the cost of the evaluation. Most psychologists, for example, do not include in the evaluation fee the cost of testifying in court or at a deposition. You can expect a psychologist to require payment in advance for testimony. And if a court date is canceled without warning, they generally charge for the time that had been reserved for the court appearance because it cannot be used.

Confidentiality

Mental health professionals adhere to confidentiality, which suggests that information will be kept private and not shared with anyone. In custody situations, however, confidentiality is not likely to be upheld. The limitations on confidentiality should be disclosed to you prior to the evaluation or at least at the beginning of it. As part of my approach to evaluations, I have each parent sign a statement indicating they understand that the results of the evaluation will NOT be confidential and will be shared with the court, attorneys, and other pertinent individuals in the evaluation process.

Parents involved in individual psychotherapy prior to the evaluation may want the content of those therapy sessions kept out of the divorce process. In such a case, you are allowed to protect your confidentiality by "invoking privilege." This means you feel the content of the therapy sessions is privileged communication and you will not sign a release for that information.

If you take this approach, the other side is likely to wonder what you are trying to hide. Some courts do not allow privilege to be invoked when a parent's mental health is called into question as part of a custody dispute. In those cases, the court may order the parent to sign a release for the information.

You must also realize that invoking privilege is generally an all or nothing situation. You cannot release the information to one person and then refuse to release it to another. For communication to be truly privileged, it must never be released to anyone.

As I said before, mental health and criminal history will also be evaluated. The extent of the history, frequency of problems, and how recently they occurred are taken into consideration. In one case, Peter, a stepfather, was being evaluated as part of a custody evaluation. It was found that he had a 14-year criminal history that included felony convictions for crimes against property and person. He had been convicted twice for sexual assault, twice for armed robbery, and had served eight years in prison. The ultimate recommendation was that the children be allowed to visit with their mother, but Peter could not be present. Furthermore, because Peter's sexual assaults had been against minors, if he ever had contact with the children, visitations with their mother would be terminated.

Psychologists view the use of collateral information in different ways. I prefer to get as much collateral information as possible to avoid surprises during court testimony. Some psychologists, however, prefer to perform the evaluation without collateral information and may or may not review it later on.

To Supervise or Not to Supervise

After weighing the data from the psychological and personality tests and interviews, a psychologist is required to render opinions based on what is in the best interest of the children. As part of this process, supervision of parental visits may be necessary. Supervision is often required in cases of substantiated abuse or if one parent is mentally ill. The process of moving from supervised visits to unsupervised visits generally follows these steps:

1. Initially, therapeutic supervised visits may occur in a therapist's office to guard against psychological harm to the children. Therapeutic supervised visits are conducted by a therapist and usually only occur for three to six sessions. In those cases where serious problems are evidenced, the supervised therapeutic visits can last indefinitely.

2. This step involves visits supervised by a disinterested third party—a person who does not have a relationship with anyone involved in the case and who may have to be paid for his or her services. Many jurisdictions have public and private agencies that have been developed for this purpose.

3. After a period of time following successful visits supervised by a disinterested third party, visits can be supervised by an interested third party—someone who is known by one or both parents and is acceptable to both of them. This could be grandparents, aunts, or uncles.

78

4. When all these steps have been completed to the satisfaction of the supervisor, guardian ad litem, court, and/or court-appointed psychologist, unsupervised visits can begin.

Completing all of these steps can take as little as several months or as long as several years. The younger the children at the beginning of supervision, and the more severe the infractions that result in supervision, the longer this process takes. Conversely, the older the children are or the less severe the infractions, the more likely it is that this process could be completed in a couple of months.

The psychologist's recommendations should also note whether therapy should be part of the process following divorce. This may include individual therapy for either or both parents and/or family therapy to deal with extended family issues. Parents often complain that extended therapy will be very costly; however, this expense is the price to be paid for being unable to come to terms without getting involved in a custody dispute.

You may want a copy of the report that is generated by the evaluation. Most psychologists are reluctant to give parents a copy of the completed report for fear it will be misunderstood or misused in the divorce action. Unfortunately, some parents take these reports and disseminate the information to friends and relatives as a way of trying to demonstrate the correctness of their position. Because of this potential for misuse, many psychologists instead write a summary letter for the parents.

The conclusions and recommendations of the psychological evaluation should include:

- Whether there should be joint or sole custody.

- Who should be the primary placement parent.

- What type of placement time the nonprimary placement parent should get.

- Whether the visits should be supervised.

- What type of therapeutic intervention, if any, is needed.

- Statements about any special circumstances in the case.

Regardless of whether you use arbitration, mediation, or litigation to resolve a custody dispute, the third party making the decision will weigh the needs of the children, the wishes of the parents, and the results of the evaluation. This information will be used to decide the best placement for the children.

Chapter 5

Two of Everything? Dealing with the Practicalities of Placement and Custody

In most custody cases, one parent is designated for primary placement of the children, although a shared placement arrangement can be made, under which children would usually spend equal time or close to equal time with each parent. Because primary placement is the norm, however, the amount of time a child should spend with the other parent needs to be determined through alternate placement schedules.

One researcher, William Hodges, established guidelines for determining the most appropriate visitation patterns. You should keep these guidelines in mind when determining how much time you would like to spend with your children and how much time you would like the other parent to spend with them. They include:

- Consider your child's developmental level in terms of what he or she needs to grow in a healthy, well-rounded manner. This should be the critera for an only child who does not need special considerations. (See the discussion following this list.)

- If you have used a visitation pattern that might seem to be developmentally inappropriate but has been successful for some time, your child is very adaptable; you should check anyway for symptoms or problems that you may have over-looked or ignored, such as difficulty at transfer, unusual dependency, and unusual detachment or spaciness. If your child exhibits no symptoms, you might be able to continue the pattern.

- If a child shows signs of attachment problems, such as difficulty separating from parents and difficulty moving from one situation to another (called transitions), consider having him or her evaluated by a mental health professional.

- If a child develops symptoms when making a transition from one parent to another, such as clinging behavior or refusing to go on a visit to a parent or grandparent, or shows symptoms in situations other than visitation, such as refusing to go to school, consider (a) that visitation problems may exist (such as psychological and/or sexual abuse, neglect, conflict); (b) that the child may be attempting to please the parent who is being left behind; and (c) that the child may find leaving the parent less painful if he or she makes everyone upset and angry.

- If a child shows symptoms such as those mentioned earlier when making a transition from both parents, consider that he or she (a) has difficulty with loss; (b) is trying to please both parents; and (c) has a difficult temperament and finds any change difficult.

- If a child is going on a parental visit with an older sibling with whom he or she has a good relationship, consider allowing longer visits.

- If the conflict between parents continues to be a problem, consider neutral transfer points for visitation, reduced frequency of transfers, and/or with the possibility of sole custody.

- If the nonprimary placement parent is mentally unstable, consider reducing visitation, frequency, and duration. Also, consider supervision or termination of parent access.
- If the nonprimary placement parent is an abuser, consider supervision or termination of visitation.
- If a child has a difficult temperament, consider increasing stability by changing the location of the visitation to a neutral setting such as a park or a grandparent's home, assuming she or he is neutral. You might also consider longer visitation times and fewer changes for added stability.
- If a child is severely alienated from a parent, consider very brief visits (30 minutes to an hour) with or without supervision.
- If parents are separated by a great geographic distance, consider frequent visits for young children if you can afford it. The primary placement parent should take the child to the nonprimary placement parent for at least half the visits, with nightly return to the primary placement parent. The rest of the time, the nonprimary placement parent should travel to the city of the primary placement parent. Also, avoid long visits with very young children. Children older than seven tolerate longer visits better.
- If a long time has passed since a child has seen a parent, but you or your child want to renew contact, consider phasing in a schedule to allow the child to get used to the other parent and rebuild trust. If neither the child nor the primary placement parent trusts the other parent, consider supervised phase-in visits.
- If the custodial parent spends a lot of time doing chores and driving car pools, is under stress, has few friends or relatives to share child care, and has a low income, he or she may benefit from some help with child care responsibilities from the noncustodial parent. Consider increased visitation times.
- If a child has an easy temperament and adjusts well to changes, and you want to change the visitation schedule,

consider how it will affect the child before you make the change. Too often, parents create and change visitation schedules based on what is convenient for them rather than on a child's welfare. What's more, a parent is more likely to overlook how a change will affect an easygoing child.

Whether a case is tried in court or mediated, or whether an agreement is reached through stipulation, a placement schedule must be developed. One of the most common and time-tested visitation schedules is every other weekend with the noncustodial parent.

The amount of time each child physically spends with his or her parents can vary. The traditional arrangement allows for an 11/3 split—the nonprimary placement parent has the children on alternate weekends and one day during the off week, or 3 out of every 14 days. Placement schedules can be made on an 11/3, 10/4, 9/5, 8/6, or 7/7 basis.

Whenever possible, keep these decisions between you and your ex-spouse because unfortunately, when left to a judge's discretion, the best possible solution may not always occur. Although judges may be well-meaning, some of them don't understand child development enough to avoid making orders that are detrimental to children.

Other Placement Plans

As a general rule, I am not in favor of alternating plans because they tend to be confusing and disruptive for parents and children. For example, a parent might have a child on Monday, Wednesday and Friday, and the other parent has him or her on Tuesday, Thursday, and Saturday, or one parent might have a child from Sunday to Wednesday and the other parent gets him or her from Wednesday to the following Sunday. You as an adult would have difficulty moving this often, so think of what it does to your children.

I recommend schedules that allow a child to have a sense of home and permanency. If parents want to work out a schedule

	Mon.	Tues.	Wed.	Thurs.	Fri.	Sat.	Sun.
Week I	Y	Y	Y	X	X	X	X
Week 2	Y	Y	X	Y	Y	Y	Y

X = overnight at father's home
Y = overnight at mother's home

Table 5.1 9/5 Plan

that gives each parent equal time, they should let the child spend half the year with the primary placement parent and the next six months with the other parent on a primary placement basis.

Both parents have something valuable to offer their children. The traditional visitation schedule puts parents in the position of having to make one of them a "real" parent and the other a visitor. To give both parents parenting time, I developed an alternative plan that seems to have worked quite well over the years.

The plan (see Table 5.1) is an extension of the traditional visitation schedule of alternating weekends. Instead of the weekend being from Friday night to Sunday afternoon or evening, I extended it to four days, from Thursday after school or work until Monday morning when school begins. With this long weekend, a parent has to help with homework, take children to sporting and other school activities, and provide discipline. The nonprimary placement parent also has an additional contact day on the off week. This part of the schedule is called the 9/5 plan.

During nonschool time, the alternate placement parent has the child 10 out of 14 days, and the primary placement parent has him or her from the end of the day Friday until Monday morning, with one contact day during the alternate week. This plan was originally called the 9/5-10/4 flip-flop arrangement; however, Judge Patrick Madden in Milwaukee County Circuit Court labeled it the Ackerman Plan.

The Ackerman Plan gives one parent primary placement during school time (September 1 to June 1) on a 9/5 basis as described above. The other parent has primary placement of the child on a 10/4 basis during nonschool time (June 1 to September 1, Thanksgiving week, two weeks at Christmas, and one week at Easter). Using this plan, the 10/4 parent would have the children 10 out of 14 days for four months a year, and the 9/5 parent would have the child nine out of 14 days for eight months a year. The 9/5 parent actually has the children approximately 20 days per year more than the 10/4 parent.

Some people have argued that this plan gives children to the 10/4 parent for all holidays. But the 9/5 parent actually has the children for four days during the two weeks at Christmas and for two days at Thanksgiving and Easter.

When deciding which parent will have primary placement during school time and which parent will have primary placement during nonschool time, several factors should be considered. Generally, the parent who is better able to support children academically and is more available to help with homework should have primary placement.

The Ackerman Plan is only one example of a placement schedule. There are many variations, any one of which may be better suited to your lifestyle and capabilities (see Table 5.2 for other plans). Whatever plan you and your spouse decide on, you'll need to be flexible and work together.

General Rules

Parents have many factors to consider when planning visitation and holiday schedules. Following are several rules of thumb.

Holiday Placement

Because holiday placement supercedes regular placement schedules, you are required to be extremely flexible to avoid problems and confusion. For example, if your weekend to have the children falls on Christmas and the other parent has holiday placement, the other parent will get the children. Holidays are a big issue in divorce situations. Emotions run higher than usual, and your children are filled with a combination of exhilaration over anticipated celebrations and anxiety about how you will handle them. Once

	Mon.	Tues.	Wed.	Thurs.	Fri.	Sat.	Sun.
Every Week	X	X	X / Y	Y	Y	Y	Y / X

X represents days spent at the father's home
Y represents days spent at the mother's home

	Mon.	Tues.	Wed.	Thurs.	Fri.	Sat.	Sun.
Week I	Y	Y	X	X	X	X	X
Week II	Y	Y	X	X	Y	Y	Y
Week III	Y	Y	X	X	X	X	X
Week IV	Y	Y	X	X	Y	Y	Y

X represents days spent at the father's home
Y represents days spent at the mother's home

	Mon.	Tues.	Wed.	Thurs.	Fri.	Sat.	Sun.
Week I	Y	Y	Y	Y	Y	X	X
Week II	Y	Y	Y	Y	Y	Y	Y
Week III	X	X	X	X	X	Y	Y
Week IV	X	X	X	X	X	X	X

X represents days spent at the father's home
Y represents days spent at the mother's home

Table 5.2 Other Schedules

again, their feelings must be given precedence over your own. Every time a holiday comes around, I am inundated with calls from parents with placement questions and problems (remember the mother and child whose plans to go to Florida were foiled by a manipulative and spiteful ex-spouse). Children are highly sensitized to even subtle changes in your moods and to what you say about holiday plans. Work these things out ahead of time to avoid last-minute chaos and tears.

In the past visitation schedules traditionally allowed for holidays to be alternated. My preference, however, is for families to share holidays as much as possible instead of alternating them. Sharing, of course, assumes the parents live in the same city. When holidays are alternated, children lose the chance to spend holiday time with half of their extended family. Not only do they miss out on visiting with one of their parents, but also with the aunts, uncles, cousins, and grandparents on that side of the family. Most of us have fond memories of extended families getting together during holidays. When holidays are shared, children have the opportunity to develop their own fond memories of both sides of the family. Here are some suggestions that may help in your planning:

Thanksgiving   One family can have Thanksgiving dinner earlier in the day, while the other can have dinner later in the day. Children can have Thanksgiving dinner with one family and dessert with the other.

Christmas   Christmas can be divided into Christmas Eve and Christmas Day. Children can spend Christmas Eve with one parent and Christmas Day with the other. However, if both parents want to have Christmas Eve or Christmas Day, then the Christmas Eve/ Christmas Day placement can be rotated on a yearly basis.

When children reach school age, Christmas visits generally include a school vacation. At this time parents may want to take a vacation with their children but be unable to do so because of the restrictions of the visitation schedule. Winter break can be shared. For example, in odd-numbered years, the mother could have the children from beginning of vacation through Christmas Eve and the father could have them from Christmas Day until school recommences. As a result, each year one parent has the children during the majority of the break. In even-numbered years the situation would reverse.

Easter   Easter can be shared by having the children spend Easter morning and Easter brunch with one family and Easter dinner with the other family.

Fourth of July   Many activities take place on this holiday, including parades, picnics, fairs, and fireworks displays. The day could be divided so that some activities occur with one family and other activities are shared with the other.

Jewish Holidays Jewish holidays can be divided the same way. One parent could have Erev Rosh Hashanah, the other parent could have Rosh Hashanah day. The same plan can be used for Yom Kippur. If both parents want the same day, it could be alternated from year to year. With Passover, one parent could have the first seder and the other, the second seder. This could remain constant from year to year or alternated. Chanukah is a long holiday that can be easily shared.

Religious Events First communions, confirmations, and bar and bat mitzvahs are important events that should be shared by both families. Generally, religious facilities are large enough that both families could attend without having to sit with one another. Parents certainly should put their differences aside long enough to participate in these important religious events with their children.

Other Holidays Children should spend Mother's Day with their mother and Father's Day with their father. Each parent should be allowed to have contact with children on his or her own birthday. Children's birthdays are seldom celebrated on the actual birthdate. One parent can arrange for a birthday party on the weekend before the actual birthdate and the other parent on the following weekend. The child will enjoy two birthday celebrations. Memorial Day and Labor Day are considered minor holidays and can either be alternated or shared depending on the parents' wishes. Many parents look at Labor Day and Memorial Day as three-day holidays, which allows for a three-day visit.

Who Will Feed the Children

Whoever has the children at 6 P.M. is responsible for feeding them. Remember that, especially with young children, mealtime decisions are a basic concern. Don't let them hear you squabbling with your former spouse about who has to make dinner. It makes children feel unwanted, heightens their anxiety, and can trigger arguments between you and your former spouse—the last thing children want to see or need to experience any time, but especially during holidays.

Transportation

The receiving parent transports the children, so you have to make arrangements in advance for them to be picked up and dropped off at a designated place. This procedure reduces the amount of conflict that can arise over transporting children. Don't allow yourself to give into any temptations to play dirty tricks, such as showing up late or not being home at the appointed time.

Be Flexible

I can't emphasize enough the need for flexibility. Don't expect to make up time that is lost to the other parent for holiday visits. Over the course of your children's childhood, this time will even out.

Make Decisions for Your Children

Don't allow children to manipulate visitation schedules. Make decisions for the children and abide by those decisions. Encourage children to have a good time with the other parent and to share their experiences with you in a healthy, positive way when they return.

The Right of First Refusal

The other parent should have the right of first refusal for alternate placement. If it is your time for placement and you will be out of town or otherwise unavailable to take your children, before taking them anyway and then hiring a babysitter, ask the other parent if she or he wants to have them. Don't be upset, however, if the other parent has already made other plans.

Separating Children

It is generally not a good idea, when establishing placement schedules, to separate children. Parents often feel that children can be separated so that each parent has an opportunity to have a child of his or her own, so to speak. However, when children don't live with one another, they don't experience sibling rivalry, and they lose the experience of learning to share and becoming aware of someone else's needs. Even though parents don't like to be exposed to their children's sibling rivalry, it serves as a training ground for interpersonal relationships during adulthood.

Another important consideration in establishing a placement schedule is making sure that children have adequate contact with the same gender parent during adolescence. As I mentioned earlier, children ordinarily, through a natural process, gravitate to the same gender parent during adolescence. When a placement schedule does not allow for adequate contact time with that parent, certain developmental experiences are lost or reduced.

Uninterrupted Time

Children in shared or alternating placements spend the entire year moving from one parent to the other. Because of this constant shuttling, each parent should have up to two weeks of uninterrupted time during the year, which would take precedence over regular visitations, but should not be used to manipulate the schedule. This way, one or both parents can plan vacation time without worrying about the visitation schedule. Blocks of uninterrupted time should be planned well in advance to avoid conflict.

Different Cities: Creating a Visitation Road Map

Most of the suggestions already mentioned apply to situations where parents live relatively close to one another. These suggestions can hold up when they live in different cities, provided the cities are not too far apart. However, a considerable distance between the locations creates a greater likelihood for conflict. Parents living in different cities can use variations of placement

91

schedules to maximize the amount of contact between parents and children.

Unfortunately, parents living a great distance apart find it virtually impossible to share placement time during the school year. School schedules are such, however, that much contact time is available during the year. Teacher conferences, teacher planning days, teachers' conventions, President's weekend, midwinter and spring breaks, and traditional holiday times allow for flexibility and visitation. Any four-day weekend during the school year should be made available to the out-of-town nonprimary placement.

The nonprimary placement parent should be allowed to travel to the city of the primary placement parent for up to four weeks of placement time, one week at a time, during the school year. Of course, travel expenses can be a major issue. To save money, you might try to arrange to stay with a friend or relative.

You should also give the nonprimary placement parent the lion's share of summertime. It's best if you allow that parent to have the children from one week after the last child is out of school until two weeks before the first child returns to school. This arrangement allows a decompression period after school is out. In addition, it allows the children to spend a couple of weeks with the primary placement parent to get ready for school, possibly go on vacation, and decompress from their summer visit with the other parent.

These approaches allow the nonprimary placement parent living in a different city to have face-to-face contact with the children almost every month of the year if his or her personal finances and time permit. People who are self-employed or have professional careers may be in a better position to use this approach.

Transporting children from one city to another might present problems. Airlines have restrictions on how old children must be to travel alone; when children are below the required age, the parent must take them to and from his or her home. This is an added expense that may also reduce the number of contacts.

Spending Additional Time with Your Children

The nonprimary placement parent naturally wants to spend as much additional time with his or her children as possible. Time can be increased in a number of ways without changing placement or visitation schedules. A parent can be a den mother or scout leader, a team coach or car pooler. Attending athletic events, practices, recitals, and performances also provides additional contact. Being available to take children when the other parent cannot gives you more time together. And, when the nonprimary placement parent's work schedule differs from the other parent's schedule, the nonprimary placement parent can act as a resource instead of children being placed in day care or with babysitters or relatives.

Making Things Work under New Rules

By now, you realize that what I said earlier is true: If you have children, your relationship with your ex-spouse doesn't end after the divorce, the rules just change. Although the situation can be tough if the divorce was not amicable, you and your ex-spouse will need to develop a new way of communicating with one another under this new set of rules.

When parents continue to fight after the divorce, their children experience significant mental health problems, including severe acting out behavior or depression. If you can't put aside your anger for your own well-being, at least put it aside for the well-being of your children.

Don't send messages to each other via your children. Although asking children to pass along messages about visitation schedules, child support, and other matters might seem simplest or easiest, such requests put children in an impossible "monkey in the middle" situation, pressuring them and directly involving them in matters that are your province. Children actually become happier, more relaxed, and feel better when they see their parents communicating with one another and know they won't have to be messengers.

If children are to be kept out of such a negative position, you and your ex-spouse must understand and follow the rules that come into play in separation and divorce as well as the new behaviors that come with them. This adherence is crucial if you are going to make placement and visitation schedules work.

The Master Schedule

Once you have explained to the children about your divorce and reassured them that it is not their fault and that you both still love them, it is time to bring some semblance of normalcy back to the household.

This point is absolutely crucial and brings to mind a five-year-old boy named Jimmy who came to my office one day crying because he couldn't figure out where he was supposed to be, when he was supposed to be with which parent, and how he was going to finally understand it all. I sat with each of his parents and Jimmy and helped develop a master schedule that Jimmy could understand. We did this by creating a calendar for him to use. Different colors represented each parent, and each day of the week was colored in with the color of the parent whose house Jimmy would be sleeping at that night. This removed much of the anxiety from his schedule because he was able to start seeing some order in his life.

It is essential to bring as much structure and organization to children's lives as possible soon after a separation has taken place. The use of a master plan or schedule is one way to do this. When the schedule or plan is created, each parent and each child should be given a copy of it for reference until it becomes automatic. As best as you can in the beginning, adhere strictly to this schedule, making as few exceptions as is realistically possible. Once children become familiar with it, variations can be introduced and they will handle adjustments with greater ease.

A general calendar can be used for the master plan. One approach is the one we used with Jimmy—shade in various days with different colors for each parent and use both colors on a day when a transition is scheduled. If your calendar looks like a dish of rainbow sherbet, you know you have planned too many transitions for your child. Any schedule should minimize transition time and maximize time spent with each parent.

A lot of tugging, pushing, bartering, and I suppose, some manipulating takes place on both sides when creating master schedules, but children love them for a number of reasons. Little children like the colors and glitziness, but all children like them because the schedule is easily accessible and they don't have to repeatedly ask Mom or Dad for information about where, when, and with whom. The calendar isn't going to yell or snarl at them or get angry with them for asking. It's there and they can deal with it.

Once the two of you separate, it is important to maintain as many household routines and rules as possible. Stability will increase a child's feelings of security and reduce the number of new rules he or she has to learn. Don't develop temporary new rules that will only be in place for a short time, thus requiring children to learn another new set of rules later on. Changing routines and rules at this time, with all the other changes that are occurring in the family, increases the level of disruption for children.

Dr. Genevieve Clapp, a family and divorce mediator, recommends that parents develop a parenting plan as part of the divorce or separation process. She suggests many different issues that should be addressed in that plan, including:

- How will communication be handled (mail, phone, or meetings)?
- What decisions will be shared? How will they be made?
- Will you both agree to the other parent's autonomy when he or she is with the children?
- When will the children be with each parent? What will be the logistics of transferring each child? Be specific. What time? Who will transport? Will children have eaten first? Who will oversee homework? What things are expected to return with them?
- What will be done if a scheduled visit cannot take place?
- How will each holiday and school vacation be divided? Be specific about times.

- When will the child and nonresident parent talk on the phone?

- How long can each parent take the children away on vacation? How much notice should be given the other parent? Should the vacationing parent provide an itinerary and emergency phone numbers?

- Try to agree on some basic rules for both homes, for example, about bedtime, discipline, homework, and television viewing.

- How will children continue the relationship with the noncustodial parent's family? Who will go to teacher conferences, and how will information about school progress be shared?

- What activities will children continue? Dance and other lessons, summer camp? Who will pay for them?

- How will children be supported?

- How will medical, dental, child care, and college bills be paid? How will future disputes be resolved?

These questions and many others need to be answered prior to the divorce taking place. If you cannot easily sit down with each other and answer them, you must use a third party, such as a counselor, mediator, or therapist.

The Parenting Plan

Many attorneys like to have parents sign a parenting agreement as a way of indicating that they agree to follow it. This means that if the plan is signed and one parent doesn't follow it, this action could be used in future court proceedings as an indication of that parent's lack of cooperation, contempt, or lack of regard for the children's needs. As always, before you sign anything, make sure you understand the ramifications.

As part of your parenting plan, you need to determine not only what areas you will agree on, but also those areas on which you will disagree. I remember a little boy named Ricky who climbed on the hood of his mother's car, using the bumper as a step. He walked across the hood, up the front windshield, over the top of the car, down the back windshield, across the trunk and then jumped off. When his mother confronted Ricky about it, he claimed that his father allowed him to do this on his car when he visited him. Ricky's mom quietly explained that his father may allow him to do that at his house, but the rules were different at her house.

Two important messages come out of this example. One message is that children need to understand that different places have different rules. This is a concept they probably have already learned. For example, children know that different rules apply when eating at a fast food outlet than when eating at a fine restaurant. One reason parents get divorced is because they don't always see eye-to-eye on all situations, and we can assume that they won't always agree on discipline or child-rearing rules. When rules are different in different places, you should be aware of the differences and teach your children that what may be acceptable in one household might not be acceptable in the other. However, don't try to convince children that you are right and the other parent is wrong.

The other important message is CHECK IT OUT. Ricky said his father allowed him to engage in such behavior, and this angered his mother. However, before letting anger get the best of her, she called Ricky's father, who said that Ricky had seen a neighborhood child do that and the father had warned Ricky, "Don't you ever try that on my car." If Ricky's mother had not checked with his father, she would have never known that Ricky had lied and that his father actually disapproved of such behavior. By looking into it, she prevented Ricky from manipulating his parents and playing one against the other. It also gave Ricky the message that he would not be able to get away with this kind of manipulation in the future because his parents were communicating with one another.

Children feed into how their parents interact with one another. Whether in an intact family or not, children try to play one parent against the other. In a nonintact family in which the parents are not communicating, when something comes up and Mom says no and the child then asks Dad and he says yes, Mom may never know what Dad said, or she may find out and become very upset with him for undermining her authority with the child. When I tell you that parents need to communicate about their children, I realize that I'm asking you to do something outside the marriage that you may not have been able to do inside it, but this communication is critical for the benefit of your children. CHECK IT OUT.

Visits and Flexibility Work Hand in Hand

Jockeying schedules can be a nightmare if you allow it to be. Here's a classic illustration of this. Bill called his ex-wife, Sally, to tell her that the following Wednesday was the father/son soccer banquet, marking the end of the soccer season, and that he wanted to take their son Chuck to the banquet. Bill wanted to trade his scheduled Thursday visit with Chuck for Wednesday so they could attend the dinner. Sally said, "No way. You're always trying to change the schedule. We went to court and the judge ordered the schedule and that's the way it's going to be." Sadly, Chuck became a victim of his mother's anger.

Parents must understand that a visitation schedule is a general guideline with a general set of rules. However, as I said before, flexibility is one of the main concepts that must be incorporated into any schedule. Chuck's mother was not punishing her ex-husband by her actions, she was punishing Chuck by forcing him to miss the banquet. This situation illustrates how one parent's anger toward the other parent overcomes concern for the child. The appropriate response from Sally would have been, "Sure. You can take Chuck to the soccer banquet and you don't have to worry about making up the day. It will all even out in the long run."

The hardest part of parenting is seeing your children hurt and knowing there's nothing you can do about it. This happens most frequently in divorce, which is why it's so important that you try not to contribute to it. One of the biggest sources of hurt for children of divorce is disappointment, and when they are disappointed you may look for a way to compensate, such as finding something else to do. Sometimes you can't fill the void. Your children hurt and you can't do anything about it. It's true that sometimes life isn't fair.

In another situation, Tom and Beth came to me for mediation. As is true in any mediation I perform, I asked each of them what their agenda was. Tom said, "Before we can mediate anything, Beth needs to give me three days of visitation that she owes me." Beth looked at Tom in disbelief and said, "I have no recollection of ever having the children for three days that you were supposed to have them."

Tom pulled out a notebook in which he had recorded time spent with the children over the past three years. He said, "On February 2, you were 10 minutes late in bringing the children back. On March 3, you asked to have the children for an extra hour because your parents were in town." There were several pages of entries. Tom flipped to the last page and said, "All of these times over the last three years add up to 72 hours and 18 minutes that I should have gotten but I didn't."

I told Tom, "I can't believe you expended the energy necessary to keep these records when it could have been spent more productively in other ways." Beth said she was sure if she had kept a similar record, the amount of time Tom had the children when he should not have would have exceeded 72 hours. The point was well taken.

Actions like Tom's are destructive and nonproductive. Tom was still angry with Beth for several reasons, but he had better ways to express that anger than by keeping those records. He had nothing to gain by this action. Instead, he looked foolish to the attorneys, the guardian ad litem, the court, and the mediator.

Transition Times Made Easier

The most difficult part of a visitation is the transition time, when a child moves from one parent's setting to that of the other parent. Children might resist leaving one parent's home or going to the other parent, not because they don't want to visit or return home but because they don't like the transition. Many children don't like transitions of any sort. Parents can mistakenly assume that a child's crying at the time of a transition means he or she does not want to go with the other parent. Before coming to this conclusion, consider if the child has difficulty with transitions in general and that the crying is his or her way of demonstrating that difficulty.

You have many ways in which to make transitions easier for children. You should decide in advance where the transition will take place. As I said earlier, I favor the general rule that the receiving parent will pick up and drop off the children. However, parents who live some distance away from one another may have to meet each other halfway. Some parents object to driving a long way to pick up children, driving home for the visit, and then repeating the journey to take them back to the other parent. They don't realize that the driving time extends visitation time. Many of the best conversations I've had with our children occurred when I was taking them from one place to another. Children are generally relaxed when they are traveling and conversation is casual. They are not pressed to complete a conversation in a short time like they are, for example, during a telephone call. Traveling time also gives parents an opportunity to eavesdrop on their children when they talk among themselves about unimportant things that might not otherwise be discussed.

Anger Gets in the Way

Unfortunately, in some situations parents don't get along with one another well enough to prevent anger from interfering with transition times. In such situations, transition may need to take place at a neutral site. For example, one parent could drop the children off with a friend or relative 15 minutes before the other parent is to pick them up, thus avoiding a conflict. I have seen cases where the courts have had to order transitions to take place at police stations because parents could not find an effective way to transfer children without getting into an argument. Imagine how disruptive and unnatural it is for a child to have to be taken to a police station several times a month to make the transition from one parent to the other.

Overcoming Resistance

Children can directly resist transition, and parents have often asked me what they should do when they have difficulty getting a child to begin or end a visit. They ask, "Should I physically pick the child up and put him or her, kicking and screaming, into the car?"

If you experience such difficulties with transition from time to time, don't worry about them. Sometimes children just don't want to visit Dad or Mom and it has nothing to do with whether they like or love the parent, but with the physical space that parent has to offer at that time. A parent might try to manipulate the schedule based on her or his perception of a child's wishes when it's really a reflection of the child not wanting to leave the familiar environment at that time. It's more a question of what the child doesn't want to leave than what the child doesn't want to do.

I don't think children should be allowed to choose whether they want to visit a parent. If difficulties persist, consider counseling or therapy for your child to help him or her work out these problems. Don't empower young children by allowing them to make a decision about visitation. It isn't their choice. Both of you are parents and presumably you both love your children. If a child doesn't want to visit with one parent, the other should say, "I understand that you don't want to do this, but the issue is not whether you go or not, the issue is what can we do to make it better because you are going." Once children become teenagers, however, you will have more difficulty forcing them into going somewhere they really don't want to go. Be prepared to do a lot more talking and reasoning with teenagers.

During these periods, the parent who is leaving the child must make the child feel more comfortable instead of shouting and blaming the disruption on the other parent. I have been involved in cases in which parents were each pulling one arm of the child in opposite directions. The child was literally caught in the middle of an ugly situation between the parents.

The greatest resistance to transition often occurs when a change in schedule is sprung on a child and he or she has no

101

time to think about it and psychologically and physically plan for it. This includes canceling visits. Never, except in extreme emergencies, cancel visits at the last minute. One child, Julie, is in individual therapy as part of the whole conflict resolution between her parents regarding their divorce. One of the biggest problems Julie has is that her mother cancels Julie's visits with her father at the last minute. Over two months, seven visits out of eight were canceled this way. This behavior makes it difficult for Julie to visit not only her father, but also the rest of her siblings, who live with him. Whether her mother's last-minute cancellations stemmed from anger toward Julie's father, disorganization, lack of cooperation, or another issue, she didn't understand how it was affecting Julie.

Discipline is another area that can affect visitation. You should not withhold time with the other parent as a form of punishment for your children. This is not fair to them or to the other parent. Parents should also not expect punishments or discipline to be extended to each other's homes without mutual agreement. For example, if a child has been restricted to the bedroom as a punishment, you cannot expect that when the child goes to visit the other parent, the visit will start off with the child being restrcted to the bedroom, thereby finishing the punishment you doled out before the transition. However, if a child is to be punished because of a major rule infraction, such as violating curfew, shoplifting, being caught with alcohol, or starting a fire in the trash, you should discuss appropriate punishment with your ex-spouse. The two of you should decide if the punishment will be in effect at both households or just the household in which it occurred or in which the child was staying at the time.

As we saw in Ricky's case, children are less likely to try to manipulate parents when they recognize that the parents are communicating. The easiest way for parents to encourage acting out behavior and manipulation on the part of their children is to not communicate with one another. How suprised children are when they discover that their parents are talking to one another and are aware that they have been manipulated.

Dividing Property with an Eye on Details

When parents separate, they usually divide their furnishings to allow each of them to have a reasonable household for the children. However, small details are often overlooked during the division process. Remember that you are getting divorced from your spouse, not the children. Many photographs and momentos are just as important to your children as they are to both of you. Because of this, family photos should be divided between both parents. If you encounter a photograph that both parents want, have it copied. When children travel to and from parents' homes, they should be allowed to bring a picture with them. It may be a photo of a parent, pet, bedroom, or grandparents—whatever makes them feel comfortable. Compiling a small album for a child to travel with is a good way to increase his or her comfort level and help make transitions easier.

One little girl named Jenny told me that when she visited her father at Christmastime, he gave her "all sorts of neat presents." But he told her that she couldn't take them home with her; she would have to play with them only at his house. She said, "I cried when he told me that, but there wasn't anything I could do."

When you give someone a gift, it belongs to that person, not you. Giving a gift to a child and then taking it away by saying he or she can't have it all the time is destructive. The child may want to take the gift home to show the other parent out of pride, to be able to play with it and enjoy it, or to share it with friends. One of parents' common fears is that if they send a gift home with a child, he or she won't be able to bring it back on the next visit. This, too, can be a problem. If your child brings home a gift and wants to take it back during the next visit, he or she should be allowed to do so. You can give very young children a tote bag or suitcase to fill with toys to be transported between households.

Toys help children master certain developmental skills. Parents should not have to invest in separate sets of toys for both households. When parents live a great distance from one another, separate sets of toys may be unavoidable. Some toys cannot be transported back and forth on a regular basis, such as bicycles.

103

However, in most circumstances, duplication should not be necessary. Don't punish your children by not permitting them to take toys back and forth just because you are angry with your ex-spouse.

This same rule applies to sending clothes back and forth. It is difficult enough to make ends meet maintaining two households. I was involved in one case in which the mother would go to school in the middle of the day to retrieve her children's winter jackets so they couldn't wear the jackets to their father's home. In another case, the father made his children take their new tennis shoes off before they went home to their mother. Such actions turn parents' problems into children's problems, and they are usually carried out with little regard for how they affect children.

Don't Move Like a Thief in the Night

Parents move when they separate and divorce. If you are planning a move, the most important factor to keep in mind is to notify your ex-spouse as soon as possible of your new address and phone number. If a move is going to take place, your children will want to talk about it with your former partner. Don't swear them to secrecy about a proposed move because this puts too much pressure on them. A move can be a family event for children if it is handled properly.

If the move that is being considered is the actual separation at the beginning of the divorce process, avoid making it on a holiday or a birthday. Otherwise, from that point forward your children will always associate that holiday or birthday with "the day my parents got divorced" or "the day Mom (Dad) left." You should not intentionally give children a lifelong negative association.

Children should be allowed to see the parent's new home as soon as possible. Even better, encourage them to help with the move. One of the biggest mistakes parents make is moving while the children are away. How destructive it is for children to go to school, only to come home and find that Dad (Mom) has moved out of the house. One research study showed that in 40 percent of cases, parents separated and moved apart without notifying the children in advance. How will children be able to trust their parents about the future when such an important event is handled this way?

Children want to feel useful and helpful during the moving process. They can load and carry boxes, and can help with unpacking and putting things away. Remember, also, that when moving day comes and furniture is divided, it should be done according to children's needs, not just your own. For example, Mom may be sufficiently angry with Dad to only allow him to take one chair, one table, and one bed. However, she must remember that her children will also be in that environment, not just her former partner.

Parents' Rights

Parents have a number of rights by virtue of being parents. They also have rights that have been mandated by laws, generally covering such areas as their children's education, medical treatment, and religious upbringing. While you are trying to come to terms with these issues, observe one cardinal rule: don't turn your problems into your children's problems.

School Conferences

Ben and Pam, who had never found a way to effectively communicate with one another, attended Amy's kindergarten conference. The kindergarten teacher happened to be sensitive to issues surrounding divorce, so she sat between Ben and Pam. When the teacher began discussing Amy's progress, she brought out the school schedule for the parents to see. She only had one copy, which she handed to Pam. Ben grabbed it from Pam. An argument ensued, and it wasn't long before Ben and Pam were hitting each other in front of the teacher. How was that teacher ever again going to be able to interact with Amy without remembering this scene? How were school authorities ever going to be able to view either of the parents without having a negative picture of the way the parents interacted? This behavior turns the parents' problems into the school's problems.

Many schools refuse to allow divorced parents to attend the same conference because of the possibility of this kind of behavior. They ask parents to designate which of them will attend conferences, and some schools allow two separate conferences to give each parent access to information about their children.

A related question that is often raised is whether stepparents should be allowed to attend school conferences. Imagine how uncomfortable it can be for a teacher to have to address two parents and two stepparents at a conference, especially if the two sides disagree about something. As a general rule, only parents should attend school conferences. However, if the couples get along with one another, it can be advantageous to include stepparents, since they may have homework or other school-related responsibilities toward the children. It is certainly important for children to recognize that parents can put their differences aside long enough to sit together at a school conference because they care about the children's best interests.

No Time Out When School Events Are on the Calendar

Your children are likely to take part in school plays, conferences, athletic events, graduations, school dinners, and other special events as part of their normal development and growth process. It is crucial for both parents to take an avid interest in school activities and to make every effort for one or both of them to attend as many functions as possible. This has a tremendous impact on children. For example, I saw a young girl named Sherry as part of an updated custody evaluation, and she was obviously deeply depressed.

Sherry's parents had been divorced for a number of years but still had not found a way to get along with one another. Even though this animosity troubled Sherry, she became accomplished in athletics and was on the school basketball and soccer teams. Both of her parents attended athletic events, but they sat on opposite sides of the field or court. However, as problems between her parents escalated, Sherry had to ask her father to stop coming

106

to the events because she was afraid they would get into an all-out fight and embarrass her in front of her friends and teammates.

As is true in many of the cases I cite in this book, because of the disagreements between her parents, Sherry was forced into the terrible position of choosing one parent over the other. The gym, concert hall, playing field, and dining room are all large enough for parents to be able to attend school events and avoid each other or avoid conflict for the sake of their children. Even better, let the children see both parents sitting together peaceably.

When a child is made to feel that he or she has to pick one parent over the other, the relationship between the selected parent and the child is artificially improved and the relationship with the nonselected parent artificially deteriorates. It's not a real improvement based on anything concrete. As time passes and the child grows older, the artificial improvement begins to peel away because it doesn't have a solid foundation, and the once-favored parent may lose favor with the child.

A child who witnesses escalating anger between parents—to the point where they become verbally or physically abusive, engaging in pushing, calling each other names, and throwing things at one another—not only becomes very upset but may also become fearful of the parent who instigates the violence. If the child perceives both parents as instigators, the relationship between them and the child will deteriorate.

Lying to your children or involving them in lies is also a way to undermine your relationship with them. For example, in Michelle's case (see Chapter 4), her mother (who was trying to keep custody away from her ex-husband) panicked before a trial date because things were not looking very good for her, and she reported to police that Michelle's father was physically abusing the child. When the police spoke with eight-year-old Michelle, she told them that she had no idea what her mother was talking about, and that she had never said any such thing. This undermined the relationship between Michelle and her mother because even a child of Michelle's age can figure out what her mother was doing. Michelle had been a strong ally of her mother, but she had trouble understanding why her mom would do something like that.

The attachments between parents and their children can go through a polarization process, during which the parents' relationships with their children change as their own relationship changes. Michelle's relationship with her father deteriorated as her mother became more angry with him. Michelle had decided that she was safer being on her mother's side because her mother assured Michelle that she would win custody of her. When relationships change, sometimes they are salvageable and sometimes they are not.

Children often tell me that Dad says one thing and Mom says another and they don't know who to believe. I never tell them to believe one or the other. I tell them to look at the behavior of both parents. Children can believe parents who do what they say they are going to do. Children just watch their parents' behavior, and over time they recognize the parent who is more honest and more even tempered. Even if children are not instructed to do this, they eventually figure it out.

Records

I can think of no circumstance in which school or medical records should be legitimately withheld from either parent. You can very easily tell a doctor or the school that you are divorced and that two copies of each record or report should be made and one sent to each parent. Don't create animosity by trying to have important records withheld from your ex-spouse. He or she has a right to know how the children are performing in school and if they are healthy.

Both of you should know about children's illnesses. From time to time, emergencies may arise and it may not be possible to notify the other parent immediately. A parent may also find it necessary to make emergency decisions before the other parent can be notified; however, such circumstances are rare. Remember that in a time of medical emergency, children can be soothed by the presence of both parents, so you should try to reach each the other as soon as possible.

Parents may disagree about whether a child should undergo a particular medical treatment. In my experience, this occurs most often with illnesses such as Attention Deficit Hyperactive Disorder (ADHD), allergies, and asthma, for which medications or treatments may have uncertain or questionable results or in which the illness itself is vague or easily misunderstood. One parent may favor using medication while the other will disclaim the illness and refuse to administer medication. Such situations can go so far that each parent has a separate doctor to support his or her position.

In the meantime, you may be exposing your child to repeated testing and examinations and perhaps even different types of medication. I have known children who were subjected to duplicate eye examinations, dental examinations, and physicals. I have seen parents throw away eyeglasses purchased by former spouses. I have even seen parents take children for a repeat of a complete psychological evaluation because they were afraid to trust the results of an evaluation obtained by the other parent. Your child is much better off if you and your former spouse can find common ground, agree to disagree if that is the case, and reach some resolution rather than subject your child to duplicate medical services.

College Education

As I said earlier, stipulated agreements or court orders that are signed at the time of a divorce often do not include provisions for college education. I have been involved in cases in which as much as $180,000 has been spent unnecessarily on attorney's fees for protracted custody battles. In some of those cases, the children's opportunity to go to college was seriously jeopardized because of the amount of money spent on the legal process.

It is deeply saddening when children finally are ready for college and they discover there is no money for tuition. Financial assistance and scholarships are available, but if parents' credit has been sufficiently damaged in the divorce process, those monies might not be accessible to their children. This problem can be avoided in many cases by making some provisions for college savings at the time of the divorce. For example, support payments can be reduced and the difference put into a trust or escrow account for college, or all or part of the money netted from selling the family home can be put into a college fund.

Religious Training

Numerous conflicts arise between parents over religious training for children. These arguments tend to escalate when parents have different religious backgrounds and did not stipulate prior to the divorce and/or separation what form the religious training should take. You are being unfair to your children when each of you takes them to different places of worship and you argue about which is most appropriate.

In one case, John grew up in a household in which his father was Jewish and his mother was Catholic. After they divorced, his father took him to synagogue on Saturday mornings and his mother took him to mass on Sundays. As John grew, he resented this so much that he rejected religion. When he reached adulthood, he embraced no religious affiliation. In another case, Christine refused to visit her father because he would not take her to confirmation class, which fell during his visitation time.

How unfortunate that a disagreement between you and your former partner may result in your children having no religious affiliation or may prevent them from realizing religious milestones. Regardless of your convictions, you must remember that much of the moral and ethical education that children receive comes from religious school and worship experiences. One or both of you refusing to cooperate in this process puts additional strain on your relationship with each other and with your children.

Phone Calls

Telephone calls between children and the nonprimary placement parent are very important. However, they must be handled in a reasonable and responsible way. I have been involved in cases in which parents called their children 5 to 10 times a day; cases in which parents insisted their children talk on the telephone for 30 to 45 minutes; cases in which parents refused to allow children to take calls from ex-spouses, saying the children were busy, playing, or doing homework.

Phone contact must be accomplished under appropriate guidelines. Except in emergencies, you do not need to speak with your child by phone more than once a day. Even when you are only calling once a day, you may encounter times when your children, especially the younger ones, simply aren't interested in speaking on the phone.

Denying children phone contact with the other parent on a regular basis can be detrimental because children need to know that Dad or Mom is just a phone call away, and that they can speak with that parent anytime they need to, especially if parents live a great distance apart. Occasionally, children will want to speak with their parent during nonscheduled phone times. As long as they are not using this as a means of avoiding responsibilities, they should have this access. Speed dial can be taught to very young children who are incapable of remembering or dialing a series of numbers.

One approach to dealing with children's need for phone time with the nonprimary placement parent is having a second telephone line for that purpose. If that phone rings and the children are not home, an answering machine can take messages for them. If children want to call the other parent, they can do so without fear of reprimand. The responsibility of making sure that this is not abused falls to both parents.

Phone calls between you and your ex-spouse should not be used as a weapon or a means of playing dirty tricks. One example of this was in an ongoing custody dispute case involving a couple named Lee and Sheila. Several times Sheila had made it difficult for Lee to have contact with their children. At one point, Sheila wanted to ask Lee to change placement times but she was certain he would not agree to it. She called him, put him on the speakerphone in front of all the children, and then asked him for a change in the schedule. This stunt was a blatant misuse of phone communication, and it put Lee in a lose/lose situation.

Phone calls should not be put on speakerphones, should not be recorded without instructions from attorneys or courts, and should not be interrupted by extraneous behavior, such as distracting children by asking them questions or having them perform unimportant tasks. Sheila had done this to Lee, repeatedly interrupting his calls to their children by giving them things to do, having discussions with them, and reminding them of chores.

In this case, for a number of reasons, placement was transferred from Sheila to Lee, and she continued to misuse telephone calls. For example, she would allow the children to call her between one and two o'clock in the morning and spend a considerable amount of time talking, using the excuse, "If my children need me, I will talk to them." It would have been just as appropriate for her to say, "I understand you would like to talk to me, but we must do this during normal waking hours." On one occasion, she stayed on a call with her children for six hours, claiming they needed to talk to her that long. Sheila did not recognize that it was actually she who needed the contact for that duration.

All of this resulted in the court ordering one telephone contact per day, not to exceed 30 minutes, if the call was made by the children and three phone contacts per week if the calls were made by Sheila. As I have said before, parental actions like Sheila's often backfire, and the parents end up with less contact with their children than they might have had if they had controlled themselves.

Presents

Children usually enjoy giving presents to their parents on birthdays, Mother's Day and Father's Day, holidays, or for anniversaries. Even if they can't give gifts, they should be allowed to send cards. You need to remind your children of these occasions for the other parent and help them select and send cards and/or presents. Although you may still be angry with your ex-spouse, your children aren't; this is another time when you have to set that anger aside for their sake. Remember, if you cooperate in helping children obtain these things for the other parent, that parent is more likely to cooperate in helping them do the same for you.

Vacations

Vacations between parents and very young children should be kept to no more than five days because when young children start missing home, they become anxious and irritable, and soon the experience may become unpleasant for you and them. As children grow older, they can handle vacations of two weeks or more.

Vacations should be planned in advance, with plenty of communication between parents about when they will occur and other details. As children grow, you must consider summertime activities when planning vacations. Don't fall into the trap of planning so many activities that it's impossible for the other parent to have any vacation time with the children. Children may come to resent your interfering with their time with their other parent. In addition, if the issue ever went to court, the court is likely to hold this against you. Just as you should allow children to cart toys and clothes between your households, you should also allow them to take a few photographs, stuffed animals, and other comforting mementos on vacation with you.

Finances

The two things parents argue about most after separation and divorce are finances and time with the children. Many states have statutory requirements regulating the amount of support that should be provided for children. In those cases, parents have no choice about how much they pay. Remember, you are supporting your children, not the other parent. One of the most difficult aspects of these controversies is when children are brought into them. I cannot begin to count the number of children who have told me, as part of a custody evaluation, how much their parents earn, how much support is being paid, who gets the deductions, how much in arrears one parent might be, and other financial facts.

Children may want to know this information but they do not need to be told it. Allowing children to have access to such information is destructive and unwarranted because it elevates the children more to the level of an adult, puts additional burdens on them, and may even draw them into arguments with their parents. Oftentimes when custody recommendations are being made, parents who provide such information to their children are viewed negatively by the custody evaluator, guardian ad litem, and/or the court.

When children ask questions about this information, you should merely say, "I understand your interest in money, but this is an adult issue. Your mother (father) and I will do whatever is best for you and you don't have to worry about it." Initially, children will worry about these issues anyway. However, as time passes and new history is made, they recognize that they have no need to worry because their parents are handling the financial concerns.

Parents Working after a Divorce

When a parent has not had to work prior to a divorce and is required to work after one, children will have greater adjustment problems than if both parents were working prior to the divorce. Psychologically, children can feel like they have lost a second parent. Divorce may necessitate a parent working part-time after never having worked before, or going from part-time to full-time employment to support or help support the household.

Work schedules should be considered when determining placement schedules. A situation in which one parent must get a child up at 4:30 or 5:00 A.M. to prepare the child for preschool, day care, or school and then go to work, but the other parent would not have to get the child up until 6:30 or 7:00 A.M., is taken into consideration in the decision-making process. However, this situation is not a major item and will not outweigh more serious concerns.

None of this is easy and if this is the first time you are getting divorced and dealing with custody and placement issues, it can be terrifying new ground to cover. However, learning to efficiently deal with this myriad of scheduling and placement concerns will actually benefit you as you move through the divorce and custody processes because you will be better able to handle some of the other pitfalls that lie ahead.

▼
Chapter

6

How to Parent Apart

Parenting in an intact family can be exhausting and exasperating at times, so imagine how challenging parenting apart can be, especially if your children are adolescents or teenagers and you have been parenting as a couple for a long time. Even if your ex-spouse wasn't an especially active parenting partner, at least he or she lived under the same roof and may have occasionally shared in decisions, discipline, homework, and other responsibilities that parents have toward their children.

As with many other facets of separation and divorce, parenting apart has its own set of rules, adjustment period, and characteristic problems, centering on maintaining two separate households with two distinct adult schedules and I hope, by now, a master schedule for the children.

You must be as flexible and communicative when parenting apart as I have asked you to be in other aspects of life during and after the divorce process. Being as preemptive as possible and nipping problems in the bud can put you in a much better position to develop a positive attitude toward parenting apart and to avoid the aggravation and emotional upheaval associated with dealing with full-blown problems.

Don't be afraid to share the responsibilities of parenting with your ex-partner simply because he or she no longer lives under the same roof. You may feel as if you are losing an element of control because not all parenting will be done under your watchful eyes, but if you are vigilant and keep lines of communication open (as did Ricky's parents), you and your former spouse should be able to find common ground for parenting even though you are apart.

Parenting apart has some plus sides, which can be especially welcome during this stressful time in your life. Both of you will come to value time you have alone without your children. Even parents living together in an intact family often ask each other to occupy the children from time to time so that tasks can be performed, errands can be run, or some quiet time can be enjoyed. This is also true when parents are separated or divorced.

During this time, it is important for parents to provide children with an environment that allows them to continue to express their love for both of you and to spend private time with each of you. You should tell your children, as many times as is necessary, that you love them and will continue loving them, regardless of what is happening between you and their other parent. These initial stages of divorce are fraught with doubts on the part of children, wondering if the love that has been present in the past will continue in the future. It is much better for you to err in the direction of telling your children too often that you love them instead of erring in the direction of not telling them enough.

The Family Conference: Increasing Avenues of Communication

Because it is inevitable that conflicts will arise within the family structure, with or without the other parent, the family conference approach is valuable to deal with all areas of concern. It opens lines of communication, gives you both a forum in which to share ideas and discuss problems, and allows children to see that you are actively dealing with issues that concern them. I recommend that family conferences take place at least once a week with participation by all members of the family who live together. Each week a different family member is designated as the recording secretary to take notes about what is discussed. These notes provide future reference if any questions arise about what was discussed or what decisions were made during conferences. Obviously, very young children should be excluded from note-taking responsibilities.

A number of rules apply to family conferences. Name-calling, shouting, and derogatory statements are not allowed. Anything a child discloses during one of these conferences should not be held against him or her in the future. Family conferences are opportunities for children to express concerns without having to worry about reprisal at a later time. If an issue arises during a family conference that involves the parent who is not present, you should communicate that information to that parent, or he or she should be invited to a future family conference to discuss the matter.

A United Front

When dealing with problems, either in a family conference or another setting, parents should, as much as possible, try to present a united front. As I said before, you don't want to leave room for a child to manipulate a situation and get away with unacceptable behavior. Bear in mind, also, that reasonable people sometimes disagree and you may end up with different rules in different settings for the same set of circumstances. If this happens, make sure your children know the different rules so they have reasonable expectations and can respond reasonably.

119

Making Visits Better

It is not unusual for children to complain to one parent that they don't like visiting the other because it is "boring." You can expect to hear complaints such as, "All Dad does is sit and watch sports on television," or "All Mom does is talk on the telephone to her friends." It is not unusual for the parent who has moved out of the family home to have an inferior or less desirable household, which may be a turnoff to children. Our home may not offer as much space or as many opportunities for entertainment or as much furniture as the other home does. Children can be very critical of this, even to the point of hurting your feelings, although often not deliberately.

When trying to deal with a situation in which one dwelling is less desirable than the other, do not try to compensate by becoming a "Disneyland parent." The Disneyland parent always tries to make life very attractive for the children by taking them places, buying things for them, or giving them privileges that may not otherwise be available. Not only can this become financially costly, but it can cost children in terms of what they expect from you as well as give them an unrealistic perception of the world. In addition, when you become a Disneyland parent, you either neglect or have less time for necessary parenting activities such as disciplining, running errands, and doing homework. As time progresses, the cost of being a Disneyland parent becomes prohibitive.

Visits can be made more desirable to children without becoming this kind of parent:

- Allow children to invite friends or younger relatives, such as cousins, to spend the entire visitation time, or at least part of it, with you.

- Let children be actively involved in planning visits. Talk to them about what will be done, where it will be done, who will be there, and how long the visit will last.

- Remember that in most visits your children will be with you for a relatively short time. Pay attention to them and their

120

desires, even if this means giving up television or telephone time. Make that sacrifice for their sake.

Loyalties

Loyalties can be a big issue in separation and divorce situations. In one case, Dick lived with his mother full-time and visited his father on alternate weekends. His mother cooked meals, did his laundry, took him to soccer practice, helped with his homework, and listened to his problems. However, whenever Dick's parents argued over issues concerning him, they vented in front of him or about each other to him and Dick felt caught in the middle. Because his mother was such a primary provider in terms of time and tasks, Dick felt it was safer for him to ally himself with her than to risk losing all she did for him by siding with his father. This occurred not because he liked his mother better, but because he was afraid of alienating her if he didn't side with her.

This is called a loyalty issue. Unfortunately, loyalty issues can escalate to where they become out of control. This most often happens with children between the ages of 9 and 12 and is called alienation. Psychiatrist Richard Gardner calls this phenomenon the Parental Alienation Syndrome. Professionals who deal with separation and divorce disagree about whether Parental Alienation Syndrome actually exists. However, I believe alienation does occur and should be noted. Gardner says that Parental Alienation Syndrome is a disturbance in which children become preoccupied with the deprecation and criticism of a parent when it is unjustified and/or exaggerated. In my experience, a majority of alienation cases have involved mothers alienating fathers from their children. However, some cases involving fathers alienating children from their mothers do occur.

In alienation cases, children are typically obsessed with hatred of the alienated parent. They talk about that parent with negative comments and profanity without embarrassment or guilt. Because this hatred generally has no basis in fact, children use trivial reasons to explain hating the other parent as a way of jus-

121

tifying the alienation. They may actually be somewhat manipulative in this process, demonstrating their hatred for the other parent only in the presence of the "loved" parent. This hatred can extend to grandparents, aunts, uncles, and close friends of the hated parent. As part of the alienation, children don't acknowledge greeting cards, they refuse gifts, and they hang up on phone calls. They also tend to blindly accept the allegations of the "loved" parent against the hated parent.

Ken was being evaluated in my office as part of a custody determination dispute. On many occasions, he had spoken about how much he hated his father, but he was unable to specifically identify what he hated. During several meetings, Ken realized that I was repeatedly asking him what was so hateful about his father. During one meeting, he finally said that he hated his father because his father bribed him. When I asked how his father did that, he gave me an example from a visit they had the night before. He said, "On the way home from my father's house, he bribed me by stopping to get a custard." Although I explained that this was typical parental behavior, whether they are involved in a divorce or not, Ken was unable to recognize that this was anything short of a hateful act on the part of his father. Children in these situations tend to view both the hated parent and the loved parent from a black/white, either/or perspective.

Alienation develops for many reasons. The most obvious is that one parent is brainwashing a child, which can involve consciously programming him or her against the other parent. When doing this, the loved parent begins an unrelenting campaign against the other parent. Mothers, for example, may complain about lack of financial support from the father, express fears about going without food, clothing, or shelter, or exaggerate minor problems with the father, such as defining infrequent drinking as alcoholic behavior.

An alienating parent makes such statements as, "After all these years, he's finally gotten around to taking you shopping." A parent may try to distance the alienated parent by refusing to share school and medical reports and records, or by not allowing the parent to attend teacher conferences. This is followed by the claim that the other parent is not interested in these things. When a parent interferes with phone contact, saying, for example, that children are busy eating or doing homework, this can be a component of alienation.

The programming of children against a parent is not always direct. It can be done in subtle and unconscious ways. Subtle criticisms are indirect communications that can take the form of statements such as, "There are things I could tell you about your father that would make your hair stand on end, but I'm not the kind of person who criticizes parents to children" or "What do you mean you want to visit your mother? Oh, what am I saying? I shouldn't have said that. I really shouldn't discourage you from seeing your mother."

Moving a considerable distance away from the other parent is another way to cause alienation. Such a move can be used to almost completely remove that parent from the child's life. A parent who alienates the other is often much less loving of the children than actions would indicate because a truly loving parent would appreciate the importance of the children's relationship with the noncustodial parent.

Emotional factors, which get back to the loyalty issue, can also lead to alienation. If a child's bond with the loved parent is stronger than with the hated parent, the child may fear that the loved parent will become angry about his or her relationship with the hated parent and may feel that it is safer to identify with the loved parent. In such a case, the child does not hate the alienated parent, but is afraid of losing the loved parent's affection.

The longer a child remains with one parent, the more the child will resist moving to the other parent. The child may say that he or she doesn't want to visit the other parent anymore and the alienating parent responds by encouraging the child not to visit rather than by being supportive. When a child objects to visiting a parent, the appropriate response is for the other parent to say, "I know you don't want to visit your father (mother), but he (she) loves you very much and wants to be with you and so the visits must continue. Maybe we can find a way together to make the visits more fun."

When alienation occurs, many things need to be done. One of the most obvious is for the family to become involved in family therapy. However, in severe cases, it may be necessary for a child to be removed from the household of the alienating parent and placed with the hated parent. Although this action is severe, in some cases it may be the only way to break the alienation process.

The final stage of this alienation process is very interesting—in most cases, children turn away from the alienating (loved) parent and toward the alienated (hated) parent. Children eventually become angrier with the alienating parent than they ever were with the alienated parent for pressuring them into hating the other parent for no good reason. For example, during a visit to my office, Gary told me that his son, Curt, who was 11 years old, didn't want to visit him. His son called him names, said he hated Gary, and misinterpreted everything Gary said and did. The court-appointed psychologist in the case suspected that Curt's mother was alienating him from his father. I told Gary that nothing much could be done if the court was not willing to take action. However, I also told him that as Curt grew older, at about 15 or 16 years of age, the likelihood was great that he would reverse his feelings and become angry with his mother. Gary accepted this, but lamented that he would miss having a relationship with his son during some of Curt's developmental years.

When Curt turned 16, he recognized that his mother had alienated him from his father. He ran away from his mother's home several times and eventually moved in with his father permanently. Now in his early 20s, Curt has a much closer relationship with his father than he does with his mother.

Power to the Children

Parents can make a big mistake by empowering children in areas where children should not have much say because of their age and ability to understand abstract issues. A classic example of this can be seen in Susan, who came to me after having been ordered by the court to undergo therapy because she had allowed her five-year-old son to decide whether he visited his father.

Children do not start developing the ability for abstract thinking until they are about 11 years old, and they do not completely develop this ability until they are about 15. As a result, directly incorporating children under 11 in the visitation decision-making process is grossly inappropriate. You can listen to the wishes of children between the ages of 11 and 15, but visitation decisions should not be made solely on the basis of what they want. One of the dangers of giving a child this much power at such an early age is what occurs during adolescence. Because these children are already accustomed to making decisions that they should not ordinarily make, they expect to do the same thing during adolescence, making decisions you may not want them to make about sexual activity, alcohol consumption, and leaving home.

A judge is not likely to order a child aged 16 or 17 to have visitation or placement that is opposed to his or her wishes. Exceptions would be made under extraordinary circumstances such as unacceptable and/or harmful behavior like alcohol or drug abuse.

Children as Coequals

Your partner has moved out. You have relied on him or her for years to help make important and minor decisions. In this scenario, you may unknowingly find relief in relying on your children to fill that same comfortable role that had been filled by your ex-spouse. Children become overburdened when they are used as confidants about financial matters, relationships, or work-related problems. Even if your child volunteers to fill that role, wanting to talk about such crucial matters, you must realize that it is better not to familiarize him or her with details of adult problems. When children ask about these issues, just say, "That is an adult matter and you do not need to be concerned about it."

Children have told me that their parents have asked them such questions as:

- Should I go to bed with my new friend?
- Should I take your mother or father to court for back support?
- Should I quit my job?

125

- Should I accept my friend's proposal?

Asking a child to respond to these concerns leads to pseudomaturity, which then leads to the same kinds of problems associated with giving a child too much power too early.

Children weathering the divorce process can also become overburdened when they feel too responsible for their own upbringing. Children who have to cook their own meals, do their laundry, care for younger siblings, and do household chores before they are physically or emotionally ready to do so can feel overwhelmed and terribly overburdened. This can cause deep mood swings, can alter performance in school if children are extremely tired from responsibilities at home, and can increase their anxiety and frustration.

Sleeping Arrangements

Children should not sleep with their parents, and they should not be allowed to start sleeping with them after separation or divorce as a way of providing extra nurturance or support or because you feel sorry for them. Allowing a child to start sleeping with you after the other parent has moved out can be psychologically dangerous. This behavior sends a mixed message to children and could lead to them becoming more insecure than separation or divorce would normally make them. You can also create feelings of rejection if you allow them to sleep with you for a while and then suddenly try to rescind permission. In extreme situations, this behavior can cause children to fantasize that they are able to replace the absent parent in the parental bed. Although such an extreme response is unusual, it can occur and so this behavior should be avoided.

As is true in intact families, children can be allowed to sleep in your bed under special circumstances (something has frightened them, such as a thunderstorm or nightmare, and they come to you seeking comfort). However, when this occurs you should explain to your child that this is an exception, not a rule, and that when the exception has ended, the child will go back to sleeping in his or her own bed. If a child expresses fear about sleeping alone after separation or divorce, you should soothe your child in his or her own bedroom. Lights can be left on, radios or tapes can be softly played, or you can comfort him or her by reading stories in the child's bedroom.

Children in the Middle

Mike and Judy came to my office to have me mediate differences between them involving their child, Emily, who was two and a half years old. During one of our meetings, both parents were enraged over an incident that had occurred the day before. Mike said that he had returned Emily with an ice cream cone at three o'clock in the afternoon. He said Judy became so angry because he had given Emily ice cream at that time that she grabbed the cone and crushed it on Mike's chest. Judy said that wasn't what had happened and in her version of the incident Mike became so angry when she had suggested the ice cream might ruin Emily's dinner that he grabbed the cone from the child's hand and crushed it on Judy's chest. Mike and Judy spent 30 minutes in my office arguing about which version was correct. They invited me to speak with Emily, with neighbors who had witnessed it, and with a friend who was sitting in Mike's car at the time.

I said it didn't matter who had crushed the ice cream cone—what was of greater concern was that Emily had been caught in the middle and had witnessed her parents acting this way. But my comments were lost on Mike and Judy and they continued arguing until I finally asked them to leave.

Another way that parents put their children between them, which I have already mentioned, is by requiring them to carry written or oral messages back and forth. Parents' anger toward each other can become so intense that they don't recognize when they are putting their children in the middle and what detrimental effects this can have on the children.

French Fries versus Mashed Potatoes

In one of my cases, an 11-year-old named Tara told me that she was making decisions about where she was going to eat based on what each parent was serving. The night before our meeting, for example, she had spoken with her mother, who was serving meat with mashed potatoes. Tara's father was serving meat with french fries. Since she liked french fries better than mashed potatoes, Tara decided to eat at his house, which he allowed. She said that her parents competed with one another over who was going to serve the more desirable meal in an effort to woo Tara to each of their homes.

We should not be surprised that Tara ended up with a perverted sense of judgment. What her parents did amounted to bribery. It is certainly all right for children to move freely from one parent's house to the other; however, the motivation for the movement is important. Two different levels of emotion were at play in Tara's situation: her parents allowed her to manipulate them, and she was given such decision-making power that it extended to every other facet of her life, including whether she went to school, what clothes were bought for her, and who she was going to be friends with. This child insisted on having such total control over her own life that she would get into screaming matches with her mother in front of their home over french fries. Her mother would warn, "If you go to your father's house, you're never coming back" and Tara would scream back, "You hate me!" and so on. Tara would go to her father's house and he would let her do anything she wanted because he didn't want to argue with her.

If you are in the process of creating a monster like this, you have to get back to one of the main rules of thumb: WINNING IS NEVER MORE IMPORTANT THAN WHAT IS BEST FOR YOUR CHILD. The best way of stopping this process is for both parents to start working together for the good of their child. If, for example, Tara's father would take a stand, saying, "You can come over here, but you're not getting dinner because you're supposed to be eating at your mother's house," Tara would start backing off. However, as long as her parents remain at odds and continue battling each other and Tara for her attention and time, Tara will continue to act out of control. The best solution is for you to hold your ground and let the child see that the parents can communicate effectively with one another.

Another french fries or mashed potatoes situation can occur when children learn that one parent is more permissive than the other. As I mentioned before, virtually all parents in intact families have experienced children playing one parent against the other. Why assume that anything different will occur in nonintact families? Children who learn that one parent is more permissive while the other is more restrictive will seek out the permissive parent whenever they want something. Children get away with this behavior repeatedly because you and your ex-partner are not communicating adequately with one another, and the children know it.

A Different Sort of Communication

Parents in the throes of divorce often ask their children about what's happening in the other household. Unless you have good reason for concern, this is another taboo. Don't pump your children for information about the other household. One case I recall involved an eight-year-old named Todd, who came to my office complaining that he did not like to visit his father. When I asked why, Todd blurted out, "Because he asks me so many questions. He asks me if the house is clean enough. He asks if we eat enough. He wants to know if my mother is dating. He asks me what her boyfriend's name is. He asks if her boyfriend stays over. He wants to know what time I go to sleep. He asks me what movies I watch . . .," and he went on and on.

You will find out over time what happens in each other's households just by listening to your children and having normal conversations with them. Children generally share information if we have patience. They may not do it as quickly as we would like or when we would like, but they will talk if you give them the opportunity through personal and phone contact.

If you have more than one child and your visitation time is limited, you may occasionally find it necessary to visit with each child alone to give him or her time to talk. These private conversations provide a special kind of quality time, allow a child to confide in you beyond the earshot of siblings, and can be special problem-solving time.

When speaking with your children, you can ask general things about their visits with the other parent, such as what they did or where they went and if they had a good time. However, don't expect them to grind out every small detail. Tell your children that if they want to discuss any of what happened during the visit, they should feel free to do so, then drop the subject until they bring it up.

Another element of communication involves how you speak to your children—the terminology you use and how you explain what's happening in the family. For example, one of my clients was an eight-year-old boy who came into my office wanting to discuss "primary placement." This term is not part of an eight-year-old's vocabulary. But when parents are telling children too much or are communicating with them on an adult level, children speak like junior adults. They catch onto the lingo very quickly and will want to talk about stipulations and status conferences, only because one or both parents is giving them too much information. Communication like this is also a form of overburdening your children by making them deal with adult issues.

Fighting in Front of the Children

When I perform a custody evaluation, I have found that one wish children most frequently share with me is for their parents to stop fighting with one another. They also often say that fighting between their parents is what makes them sad or mad. Children whose parents continue to argue up to five years after the divorce are much more likely to have significant psychological problems. If you must argue with each other, do it without the children being present and where they can't hear you. And, as I said before, don't express your anger for one another through your children by actions such as withholding phone contact, interfering with visitations, or preventing children from accepting gifts.

Check It Out

CHECK IT OUT!

        CHECK IT OUT!

                CHECK IT OUT!

I cannot say often enough that you need to verify the things children say and do by checking them out with one another. This reminds me of a high school principal who said at open house, "I promise not to believe all the things your children say about your home, if you promise not to believe all they say about our school."

Children have active imaginations. They fill in blanks with fantasy when they have partial information. They distort and exaggerate facts and will take advantage of opportunities to manipulate adults. Any time your child tells you a story about something that has happened at the other household, before you believe it, check it out. To get you to approve a particular behavior or action, children will attempt to convince you that the other parent allows it, when that may not be the case. You will find this behavior especially in situations involving discipline issues, television and movie viewing, what children are allowed to eat, what their bedtime is, and who they are allowed to associate with.

Checking things out lets children know that they cannot make statements and assume you will not verify them with each other. Checking it out reduces manipulation, lying, and anger between parents.

Secrecy

Asking children to keep secrets from parents puts them in a difficult position and heightens their anxiety and stress. This is one of the pitfalls of parenting apart that I've already mentioned, but it is worth repeating.

The biggest part of the secrecy issue is that it puts so much pressure on the child. If you tell a secret to a three-year-old, he or she quickly tells somebody else because at that age, a child does not know that *secret* means not telling anybody. But older children who understand the concept of secrecy feel tremendous pressure. Secrets entrusted to children often include, "We're moving," "I have a boyfriend," "I took you to the doctor," "You're changing schools," followed by "Don't tell Mom" or "Don't tell Dad." Not only does a child have to worry about the consequences of telling the other parent, but now he or she must also keep track of what can and can't be spoken about.

Parents wonder why their children don't do well in school while advancing through the divorce process. Imagine a second grader sitting in class trying to remember what it was that she was supposed to tell Dad and what she couldn't tell him instead of listening to the teacher explain the number system.

Older children get sucked into the same thing but they become coconspirators. They learn that keeping secrets and lying by withholding information are part of the rules of being in a divorce situation and they try to invoke the rules themselves. For example, a teenager might say to a parent, "Why don't you let me go to the dance tonight and we won't tell Dad" or "You can let me sleep over at my friend's house but we don't have to tell Mom because she doesn't like my friend."

Where to Live

Separated and divorced parents should live as close to each other as is reasonably possible. This doesn't mean you have to live next door or across the street, but you should think in terms of blocks and not miles. The advantages of living close to one another far outweigh the disadvantages. This is another potential bright light for children, and one of those opportunities for parents to soften the hard times associated with divorce, if they can deal with it effectively. This arrangement gives children easier access to both of you and gives both of you easier access to each other. It makes life simpler and often removes some of the anxiety and frustration associated with visitation transition times, transportation, emergencies, and communication.

Older children can actually walk or ride a bike or bus between your homes when you live within a reasonable distance of each other. This easier access also applies to schoolwork and special projects. When parents tell me that they could not possibly live that close after separating or divorcing because they don't want to see each other all the time, I ask them, "How many neighbors do you know who live three blocks from you?"

Problems with the Other Parent

Ellen came to my office wondering what she should do about her ex-spouse, Harry, who had a pattern of disappearing and then reappearing again in her life. He had left home when their son was born, was gone for three years, then reappeared and had regular contact with the child until he was five. Harry then disappeared again. Three and a half years later he came back on the scene and Ellen did not know if she should reinstitute regular contact between him and their son.

Ellen's son remembered nothing about his father except that he kept going away. He couldn't recall anything they had done together or what the man looked like. He had even told some of his friends that his father was dead.

A number of parents follow this here-one-day-gone-the-next pattern and in those cases the question is always asked: Should they be allowed to reenter a child's life? If we could be guaranteed that a parent would reenter a child's life and keep in contact throughout childhood, we wouldn't need to ask this question. However, this constant disappearing/reappearing act may continue throughout a child's life and does not provide the kind of stability and security children need for appropriate development.

The basic message to parents is this: If you want to be part of your child's life you must be consistently available, not just when it is convenient for you. In some cases, parents have lost the right to have contact with their children because of the inconsistency of moving in and out of the children's lives.

Parents Who Won't Visit

Parents cannot be forced to visit their children. This neglect can be very damaging and frustrating for a child who longs to spend time with a mother or father who has become disinterested.

133

This is a difficult situation for the primary placement parent. How can you convince children that Mom or Dad still loves them when they don't send birthday cards or attend school concerts? On the other hand, how do you tell children that maybe the other parent doesn't love them anymore? You can't do that. But these children pick up that feeling and a shroud of sadness covers them all the time. It really is sadness. You can see it in them and feel it when you are in their presence. They are communicating, "I just don't get it." And, of course, many of them wonder what they did wrong to turn the other parent against them and what they can do to fix it.

This reminds me of a case in which the parents had their children on alternating full weekends and the father came to see me for mediation because he wanted to spend less time with his children. He wanted them only every other Saturday afternoon, but his ex-wife was pleading with him to spend more time with them and be a parental influence. The children, in the meantime, wanted to know what was wrong with their father, why he didn't call them anymore, and why he only wanted to see them for a few hours every couple of weeks. The father shared the short time that he spent with his children with his girlfriend, and the children began believing that he cared more about her than he did about them. They may have been correct.

When this sort of thing happens, you must explain to your children that you wish the other parent would spend more time with them, but, unfortunately, it is not within your control. Be as supportive as you can and reassure them of your love and dedication, but do not offer false hope that the other parent may someday increase visitation. He or she may never do that, and such failed expectations can be devastating for a child. Simply tell your children that you hope their other parent will eventually spend more time with them, but you can't make any promises. You can also try to find substitutes for your children to spend time with, such as relatives of the same gender as the parent who doesn't want to visit, or volunteers such as Big Sisters and Big Brothers.

Lack of Cooperation

I cannot begin to recount from the thousand-plus divorce-related cases with which I have been involved how many times a parent came to my office frustrated, demoralized, and reduced to tears because he or she could not obtain the cooperation of the other parent in matters pertaining to their children. I have seen cases in which parents have tried to share necessary information only to be spurned by their former partners and cases in which courts repeatedly, but to no avail, warned parents of the negative effects of lack of cooperation, undermining relationships, and acting against the best interests of their children. In spite of warnings, some parents insist on remaining uncooperative, taking a case to court a dozen times in three years, arguing, manipulating, and being more concerned about being angry with their ex-partner than doing what is best for their children.

When ex-spouses engage in this behavior, you must simply try to make the best of it. Some parents have attempted to terminate parental rights of the uncooperative parent, but courts agree to that only in rare instances when parents are guilty of dangerous or abusive behavior involving their children.

The Mentally Ill Parent

The less time a child spends with a mentally ill parent, the better off that child will be. If, during a custody evaluation, I see a parent who appears to be significantly mentally unstable, it weighs heavily against that parent.

One of the most important factors in child rearing is that the environment be predictable, stable, and safe. When living with a person who is severely mentally ill, the environment will be unpredictable, insecure, and perhaps even unsafe. It is extraordinarily difficult for children to grow up in a setting in which a particular behavior is rewarded one day, punished the next, and ignored the third. Children grow up feeling insecure, not trusting their environment, and having considerable difficulty with inter-

135

personal or close relationships. Add to this uncertainty the typical issues for a child whose parents are divorcing, such as what school he or she will attend and if basic necessities are going to be met regularly, and it can be mayhem.

The truly mentally ill parent does not communicate in a way a child can understand. In some cases, such parents are speaking languages adults can't even understand—a kind of jibberish that accompanies chronic mental illness. Children not only have difficulty communicating verbally with such parents, they are also kept off balance because they never know what mood the parent is going to be in on any given day: happy and content, aggressive and yelling, hitting and screaming, or sad and crying. At this point, the child's insecurity reaches an emotional level instead of staying on a concrete level, and that is even more devasting to a child because it is embedded in unpredictability.

In situations like this, children's whole lives are chaotic. They can't count on anything. They never feel grounded. They don't feel confident enough to raise their hands in a classroom and take the risk of answering a question, knowing it might be wrong. They withdraw and become passive, which is reflected in their school grades.

Some of these parents get into therapy with positive results. But different kinds of psychological problems exist. If someone's psychological problem, such as depression, is caused by a bodily chemical imbalance and medication can fix it, that solution is workable while the parent continues to take the medication as long as necessary. This solution is different than for a parent who has a character disorder. Parents with severe character disorders are likely to teach their children that character disorder behavior and the children have no way of understanding its consequences.

As I mentioned earlier, alcohol and drug abuse provide a similiarly unstable environment in which it is equally difficult to raise children. Parents who have a history of substance abuse but are currently clean and sober find it difficult to understand the effects that their drug- or alcohol-induced behavior had on their children. They often don't remember anything they said or did, and they must rely on their children and the other parent to accurately recount their behavior, something very painful for everyone. When parents have engaged in prolonged substance abuse, visitation time should be made contingent on random, clean drug screens. If drug screens reveal renewed abuse, visitation should be supervised or suspended until the problem is once again under control.

Living with a mentally ill parent or one who abuses drugs, alcohol, or both becomes a tremendous burden on children. If the children are old enough to understand that the parent is in trouble, they tend to feel responsible for that parent as well as for themselves and their siblings. Some children end up in role reversal, providing for the psychological stability of the parent and becoming the parent's therapist, confidant, and supporter. As soon as it is discovered that a child is in this situation, it must be rectified as quickly as possible.

The longer this type of overburdening continues, the more likely children are to develop significant depression, personal relationship problems, and/or retaliatory acting out behavior in an attempt to rebel and fight back against the burden and the parents who have allowed it. An environment like this in which children must learn to cope with the most extreme conditions simply to survive is emotionally abusive because the children are being beaten up psychologically every day of their lives.

Chapter

7

Handling Custody Problems and Disputes

Abuse and/or the potential for it are two of the major concerns in custody disputes. Reported abuse cases have increased dramatically over the last two decades and the number is continuing to rise. Between 1983 and 1991, for example, the number of reports grew by almost 1 million to 2.6 million from 1.7 million.

Contributing to these ballooning and alarming figures is heightened public awareness that abuse should not go unreported. Consequently, the number of cases being directed to child protective service agencies has risen steadily.

Physical Abuse

A major problem associated with reporting abuse is the difficulty defining what constitutes physical abuse. Many behaviors that

139

were considered acceptable punishments in the past are now thought to be abusive. For example, punishments involving hitting a child with wooden spoons, paddles, belts, and switches that leave bruises or other marks are considered physical abuse today. In fact, any type of physical intervention that causes injury or harm to the victim is classified as physical abuse.

We know that abusiveness within families does not only occur between parents and children. It also takes place between spouses and other family members, such as aunts, uncles, cousins, and grandparents, and can take place between children and these other relatives.

Let's be very clear on what the law calls abuse and neglect. The Children Abuse Prevention Act (Public Law 100-294, U.S. Department of Health and Human Services, 1992) states:

Physical or mental injury (sexual abuse or exploitation, negligent treatment or maltreatment) of a child (a person under the age of 18, unless the child protection law of the state in which the child resides specifies a younger age for cases not involving sexual abuse) by a person (including any employee of a residential facility or any staff personnel providing out-of-home care) who is responsible for the child's welfare under circumstances which indicate that the child's health or welfare is harmed or threatened thereby . . .

Physical abuse is characterized by inflicting physical injury or punching, beating, kicking, biting, burning, or otherwise harming a child. Although the injury is not an accident, the parent or caretaker may not have intended to hurt the child. The injury may have resulted from over-discipline or physical punishment that is inappropriate to the child's age . . .

Child neglect is characterized by failure to provide the child's basic needs. Neglect can be physical, educational, or emotional. The latest incidence study defines these three types of neglect as follows: physical neglect includes refusal of or delay in seeking health care, abandonment, expulsion from home, or not allowing a runaway to return, and inadequate supervision. Educational neglect is permission for chronic truancy, failure to enroll a child of mandatory school age, and inattention to a special educational need.

Who Will Be Abusers?

Considerable research has gone into attempts to predict who will be child abusers, and certain characteristics that are common among many abusers have been identified. For example, parents are more likely to maltreat their children if they:

- Use drugs or alcohol (alcoholic mothers are three times more likely and alcoholic fathers eight times more likely to abuse or neglect their children than nonalcoholic parents);
- Are isolated, with no family or friends to depend on;
- Were emotionally deprived, abused, or neglected as children;
- Feel worthless and have never been loved or cared about;
- Are in poor health.

In the Children Abuse Prevention Treatment Act, the Department of Health notes:

> Many abusive and neglectful parents do not intend to harm their children and often feel remorse about their maltreating behavior. However, their own problems may prevent them from stopping their harmful behavior and may result in resistance to outside intervention. It is important to remember that diligent and effective intervention efforts may overcome the parent's resistance and help them change their abusive and neglectful behavior.
>
> Children are more likely to be at risk of maltreatment if they are unwanted, resemble someone the parents dislike, or have physical or behavioral traits which make them different or especially difficult to care for.

A person's environment—including changes in one's financial condition, employment status, and/or family structure—can also increase the likelihood of abuse. Several general characteristics have been found in physical abusers:

- It is likely that they were physically abused as children.
- They have a higher level of reaction to the negative things that children do.

141

- They have more physical symptoms of generally poor health and more mental illnesses such as personality disorders.
- They have lower ego-strength than nonabusing parents, which contributes to them lauding physical strength over those less able to defend themselves.
- They have poorer self-concepts.
- They have difficulty controlling their own behavior and look for outside means of control, such as alcohol and drugs.
- They have greater expectations for appropriate behavior from children, experience greater stress, and have a higher frequency of depression.
- They have greater levels of anxiety than do nonabusing parents.
- They tend to feel more socially isolated.
- They have lower rates of interaction with their children.
- They rely on power as a form of discipline more than non-abusing parents do.

One of the difficulties associated with allegations of abuse is proving that the abuse actually took place. Many acts of physical and sexual abuse are perpetrated against children under the age of three, and it is difficult for them to adequately describe what has occurred. In such situations, when an eyewitness was not present, we must rely on physical evidence as a primary source of information. The rate of substantiation is declining instead of increasing over time. One reason is that funding for social services agencies, which perform these investigations, has not increased to keep up with the demanding caseload.

Consequences of Childhood Physical Abuse

In 1993, psychologists Robin Malinosky-Rummell and David Hansen published a paper reviewing the long-term consequences of childhood physical abuse. They noted that adolescents who show aggressive and violent behavior are more apt to have been physically maltreated as children than the general population. Boys in residential treatment centers and children in mental health treatment facilities were also more likely to have been physically abused than children in other groups. Additionally, higher rates of physical abuse during childhood were found among prison inmates than among noninmates.

Perhaps the most startling element of the researchers' work was the finding that one-third of individuals who were physically abused or neglected as children ended up abusing their own children. This abuse also spills over into the realm of dating, where five percent of abused individuals inflicted some form of violence on their dates.

Adults who were physically abused as children are also more likely to show violence toward their spouses. This presents an important consideration for married couples: when your partner is abusive, you must decide if you want to stay in the relationship or escape for your own good and the good of your children. Once again I'll remind you that children learn what they live. When a victim of spousal abuse stays in that relationship, he or she teaches the children in the family that it is okay to beat a partner or to be beaten up by a partner.

Physically abused children tend to be more unruly than are nonabused children, displaying more acting out behavior and disorders. A direct correlation exists between the amount and severity of physical abuse that a child endures between the ages of 2 and 12 and the amount and severity of acting out behavior that that child exhibits during adolescence. The basic message is that the more you physically abuse a child, the more he or she will act out that punishment as an adolescent. This behavior includes turning to drugs and alcohol. Thirty percent of children who have been sexually and physically abused become substance abusers during adolescence.

People who were physically abused as children are also more likely to kill or injure. They also have more emotional problems than nonabused children, including anxiety and depression, and more psychologically based physical problems, such as hostility, paranoia, and psychosis. Individuals who were physically abused as children also have poorer abilities to build and maintain per-

143

sonal relationships, and they have more academic and vocational difficulties than the general population does.

The message that springs from these research findings is simple: DON'T ABUSE YOUR CHILDREN and DON'T ALLOW YOUR CHILDREN TO BE ABUSED. Almost every aspect of a child's life is negatively impacted by physical abuse and so everything humanly possible must be done to avoid exposing children to this abuse. If you are an abuser or afraid that you will become one, get psychological help. If your spouse or partner is an abuser, get out of the relationship.

Family Violence

The U.S. Department of Health and Human Services defines family violence, or domestic violence, as:

> The use or threat of physical violence by the abuser to gain control and power over the victim. It occurs in households of both married and cohabitating couples. Although either party may be the victim, most victims are women. The three types of spouse abuse (physical abuse, sexual violence, and psychological/emotional abuse) often occur in combination.
>
> . . . Physical abuse can take many forms including kicking, hitting, biting, choking, pushing, and assaults with weapons. Sometimes particular areas are targeted, such as the abdomen of a pregnant woman.

Victims stay in abusive relationships because they blame themselves for the abuse, feeling that they deserved it, or they believe the abuse will stop. Abusers frequently make this promise, and spouses believe them. Many victims have nowhere to go and they feel that they are so financially dependent on a relationship that even though it is abusive they cannot consider leaving it. They also stay out of fear that they and their children will be seriously injured or killed if they even try to leave.

Observing family violence affects children and experiencing family violence affects adults. These victims tend to have feelings of worthlessness, a greater incidence of depression, suicidal feelings, a negative self-image, and an inability to develop trust in intimate relationships. Children raised in abusive households learn that violence toward a loved one is acceptable, and they tend to develop many symptoms of their own in response to the violence, including truancy from school, bed-wetting and difficulty sleeping. Young children often entertain the fantasy that they can do something to stop the violence, and they may actually physically attempt to intervene by jumping between the abuser and victim or pleading for it to stop, thereby endangering themselves. In 45 percent of spousal abuse cases, children are also abused.

Children living in homes with spousal abuse are two to three times more likely to have failing grades, to have difficulty forming relationships, to experience discipline problems, to engage in actual fights in school, and to exhibit such acting out behavior as vandalism, substance abuse, and sexual promiscuity.

Family violence is also linked to the frustration-aggression hypothesis, wherein the higher the frustration the greater the aggression. It's not unusual in divorce cases for each spouse to accuse the other of physical violence against him or her and then bring in character witnesses to prove the charges false. Sadly, many of them them do hit and otherwise physically abuse each other, and this activity tends to increase (and spill over to the children) with the level of frustration. Aggression directed at children because a parent is angry with the spouse but can't take it out on him or her has an even greater impact on youngsters. People who act out this behavior belong in therapy, where they can learn anger management.

A study conducted in 1990 by Lane Veltkamp and Thomas Miller summarized the long-term affects of family violence:

- Victims tend to develop self-destructive tendencies.

- Women who have been abused show significant adjustment difficulties and problems related to interpersonal and sexual relationships with males and females.

- Abuse victims tend to abuse their offspring, thereby passing along abuse to future generations.

- The most significant symptoms displayed by adults who are physically and sexually abused include depression, self-de-

145

structiveness, anxiety, traumatic stress, feelings of isolation, poor self-esteem, tendencies toward revictimization, substance abuse, difficulty trusting others, and sexual maladjustment in adulthood.

People are more likely to contribute to family violence under the following circumstances:

- They have experienced poverty.
- They have a minimal support network.
- They do not have the advantage of a family working together.
- They have a lower level of education.
- They have chronic employment problems.
- They overrely on physical punishment.
- They are rigid and inflexible.
- They are not involved with members of their extended family.

Violence is absent in households in which the family is well-integrated, people have the ability and opportunity to make their needs known, mental illness is absent, parents provide appropriate parenting skills and a supportive environment, and there is no overly dominant family member.

Emotional Abuse

The U.S. Department of Health and Human Services has said that:

A child is considered to be emotionally or psychologically abused when he or she is the subject of acts or omissions by parents or other persons responsible for the child's care that have caused, or could cause, a serious behavioral, cognitive, emotional, or mental disorder. In some cases of emotional/psychological abuse, the acts of the parents, or other caretakers, alone, without any harm to the child's behavior or condition, are sufficient to warrant Child Protective Services intervention. An example would be if the parents/

caretakers use extreme or bizarre forms of punishment such as torture or confinement of the child in a dark closet. For less severe acts, such as habitual skapegoating, belittling, or rejecting treatment, demonstrable harm to the child is often required for Child Protective Service to intervene.

An example of emotional or psychological abuse is if a parent restricts a child to his or her room any time the child is not in school as a way of not allowing contact with other children. Neglect also includes failure to provide appropriate medical treatment, permission for drug or alcohol use by a child, or failure to provide needed psychological or medical care. Any behavior in which a parent engages that interferes with a child's ability to develop appropriate self-esteem, social competence, and positive interpersonal relationships is an aspect of psychological maltreatment.

Parents may, at times, say things in jest to their children that might be construed as offensive or emotionally abusive. If something is said or threatened often enough, a child may believe that it is true or that it will occur and that belief makes the comment psychologically or emotionally abusive. Here are some things parents say that are abusive:

- Saying to a young child: "If you don't stop acting that way I'm going to leave you alone and never come back."
- Coming from a father who believes a child is not his own: "You're not mine. Get of out my sight. I don't want to have anything to do with you."
- Threatening to send a child to a foster home or detention center or threatening to pack a child's bags and make him or her leave.
- Repeatedly calling a child "dummy" or "slob" or other even less flattering names.

A parent is guilty of maltreatment when he or she is consistently unavailable to respond to children's needs or ignores or rejects the children. Maltreatment includes not meeting physical needs, failing to feed children, failing to keep them clean, and even dressing them inappropriately. Another form of maltreat-

147

ment is called infantilization, which occurs when a parent insists that a child engage in infant-like behavior or behaviors that are typical of children many years younger than the child.

In general, infants tend to be psychologically maltreated through rejection, unavailability, malnourishment, or inconsistency. Children are usually maltreated through behaviors that suggest they are unloved, unwanted, inferior, or inadequate, and through removal from their home. Adolescents tend to be mistreated in the same manner as children, but the patterns are often stronger and more elaborate.

Psychological or emotional abuse can also take the form of economic dominance or dependence. The U.S. Department of Social Services has said that abusers:

> Use the children to maintain power and control over their partners. For example, they belittle or degrade the cildren as a means of harassing the victim. Abusers may frighten their victims by using looks, actions, gestures, or loud voices; by smashing things; by destroying the victim's property. Abusers may threaten to take the children away from their spouse, to harm the children, or [to] commit suicide. Men who [use their form of] abuse may control their partner's activities, companions, or whereabouts. [They] often control what their victims do, whom they see, and where they go. Many abusers feel threatened by anyone with whom their victims have contact.

Sexual Abuse

One of the most difficult elements of proving sexual abuse is that people generally can't agree on how to define it. For example, is it sexual abuse when a child catches a glimpse of an exhibitionist? Most people would not consider it sexual abuse if a child was shown a pornographic magazine by a playmate. However, is it sexual abuse if a child is shown pornography by an adult? Does a parent sleeping with a child constitute sexual abuse in the absence of sexual touching? What if the child is a teenager and becomes aroused by sleeping with a parent? These questions are difficult to answer because they fall into a gray area; however, not all sexual abuse allegations come to rest there.

The U.S. Department of Health and Human Services defines sexual abuse as:

> Fondling of child's genitals, intercourse, incest, rape, sodomy, exhibitionism, and sexual exploitation. To be considered sexual abuse, these have to be committed by a person responsible for the care of the child (e.g., a parent, a baby-sitter, or a day care provider). If a stranger commits these acts, it would be considered sexual assault and handled solely by the police in the criminal courts.

As a result of research pertaining to sexual abusers, researcher David Finkelhor theorized that:

- Some groups of abusers have an unusual need for power and domination.
- Most groups of offenders who have been tested using psychological monitors show unusual levels of deviant sexual arousal to children.
- Many offenders were themselves victims of sexual abuse.
- Alcohol is connected to acts of sexual abuse in a large number of incidents.

Finkelhor also noted that children are at higher risk of abuse if:

- A child is living without one of his or her biological parents.
- A child's mother is unavailable either because of work outside the home, disability, or illness.
- A child reports having a poor relationship with his or her parents or is being subjected to extreme punitive discipline or child abuse.

One of the most frequently asked questions in child sexual abuse allegation cases is whether the perpetrator is likely to sexually abuse again. This is called recidivism. The greatest risk for repeat offending occurs in the first 5 to 10 years after the original offense. One study showed that 42 percent of the sexual abusers included in the survey were reconvicted of child abuse at some time. Of those reoffending individuals, 23 percent were reconvicted more than 10 years after they were released from prison.

If You Think Your Child Has Been Sexually Abused

If you suspect that your child has been sexually abused:

- Do not interrogate or question him or her;
- Listen and be supportive;
- Don't completely discount a child because the allegations involve your spouse, significant other, relative, or friend and you don't want to believe that he or she could do such a thing;
- Immediately report your suspicions to your pediatrician, the police, and/or your local child protective services agency;
- If a significant other or parent is involved, you should ask the person to live someplace else until the matter can be sorted out and the truth known. In a situation like this, it would not be appropriate for you to allow a visit with the accused offender until the child has seen a professional and arrangements have been made to safeguard the child during visitation. If the suspected offender won't leave, you and your child may have to spend a short time at a motel or with a relative until the situation is sorted out.

If you ask a child the wrong questions at the outset, you may contaminate the process; that is, you may inadvertently feed a child information. In so doing, even if sexual abuse has occurred, you may ruin the case from the legal standpoint and the offender may go free. Many times parents have come to my office with an audiotape or videotape of them interviewing a child about suspected sexual abuse. The tapes are filled with leading questions, suggestions, and inappropriate communications. Questioning in a case of this nature must be done by a well-trained professional. The best place to start is with a child protective services agency or a sexual assault treatment center, if your city has one.

Your response to an allegation of this nature is crucial to how your child deals with it. For example, if you become hysterical and make statements such as, "Oh, my God, that's the worst thing I've ever heard. You poor baby," a child's emotional response to the situation is going to be compounded. In one study, more than 100 women who had been sexually abused as children were interviewed. Two factors contributed to the feelings they had in adulthood about the abuse—one was their perception of what had occurred and the second was their mother's response to it.

After you have reported your suspicions to the proper authorities, you should quickly get your child involved in therapy. Children who are abused learn to become victims and they accept the fact that this is the way their lives are to be lived. When they grow up with that notion, they become "sitting ducks" for spousal abuse, sexual harrassment, and abuse in the workplace. Children must not be allowed to mature with the belief that it is acceptable to be a victim. The victimization cycle must be broken and the most effective way of doing that is with psychotherapy, in which a child can unlearn being a victim and unlearn victim-like behavior.

In one case in which a victim never unlearned victim-like behavior, a woman named Leslie was married for 25 years to a businessman who beat her regularly. After the beatings, he would instruct her not to leave their home until her bruises had healed. He would come home the following day and there would be no food in the house because Leslie had followed his instructions, and he would beat her because she hadn't shopped for food. After several years of psychotherapy, she recognized that she should leave the marriage and file for divorce, but she never unlearned her victim behavior. Three years after her divorce, her husband showed up at her door with a basketful of laundry and said, "Wash my clothes." She said, "Okay." He added, "While you're at it, make me lunch," and she said, "Okay."

Sexual Abuse Allegations: True or False

Ninety percent of sexual abusers don't admit to their crimes. That means that in 90 percent of the cases, someone must determine if the abuse actually occurred. When a sexual abuse allegation is made, there is a victim. The question is, who is it? Is it the child who is at the heart of the allegation or a parent who may be falsely accused? In the vast majority of cases, the allegations are true; however, in a significant minority of cases, they are false.

In the past, we relied on the amount of detail a child could provide in an effort to determine if allegations of sexual abuse were true or false. That cannot be done today. Children have access to too much information about sex and sexuality. Network and cable television, videotapes, sex education programs in school, and information exchange with other children all provide a base of sexual information that may leave a child confused, but informed. Children who have sexual knowledge have not necessarily gained it from direct sexual encounters. Even daytime television programs are filled with sexual information. I'll never forget my surprise one day when I went home to pick up something and I decided to make myself some lunch and watch television while I ate. The soap opera that was being aired showed a man and woman in bed, under a sheet. Next to the bed was a bowl of strawberries and a bowl of whipped cream. The couple was describing in graphic detail what they were going to do to each other with the strawberries and whipped cream. The only difference between what was shown on that soap opera, to which children have access, and what can be seen in an R-rated movie is that this couple was covered with a sheet.

Another factor that makes sexual abuse more difficult to determine is that most behavior resulting from sexual abuse can also be caused by ordinary problems. Nightmares, infantile behavior, excessive masturbation, and signs of depression can occur in children regardless of whether they have been sexually abused. Almost all children between the ages of three and six years masturbate, sometimes to excess. It is not uncommon for children who have never been abused to experience nightmares. And children under five may describe acceptable hygiene practiced on them by a parent in a way that sounds like sexual abuse. When children say they have been touched on their genitals, it does not necessarily mean the touching was sexual.

152

In some cases children lie about sexual abuse. This is also difficult to verify because children under five usually lack the verbal and conceptual skills necessary for them to undergo adequate psychological testing and to be able to fully coooperate with a professional interview. And the more a child is tested, the more likely it is that the results will become increasingly unreliable.

It is not good practice to use sexually anatomically correct dolls to allow children to show how sexual abuse occurred. If your child says he or she has been sexually abused, don't use dolls to have the child show you how. If the dolls are used inappropriately, prematurely, or sometimes even at all, they may sufficiently contaminate the case so that it may never go to court. The American Psychological Association warns about using such dolls in cases of alleged sexual abuse.

Almost all false sexual abuse allegations occur during custody disputes. Consequently, when such an allegation is lodged during a custody fight, everyone becomes concerned about whether it is true.

I recall one case in which a mother, who knew she was in danger of losing custody of her child, used allegations against her ex-spouse to postpone three court dates. First, she made allegations of domestic violence and the court postponed the case to investigate those charges. She then alleged that her ex-partner sexually abused their daughter and the court postponed the case to look into it. Then, one week before the third date, she alleged that her ex-husband had physically abused their child and again the court postponed the case to investigate.

Whether or not such allegations are true, they muddy up a case enough to where the court develops doubts about the parent who is being repeatedly accused of unacceptable behavior. Courts separate children from parents before they know for certain if a parent has done something grossly inappropriate.

It is, however, extremely difficult for a parent to succeed at initiating a false sexual abuse allegation and be able to carry it out. It would require considerable memorization on the part of a child, and parents cannot successfully coach a child to appropriately answer all the questions of social workers, psychologists, police, guardians ad litem, and the courts. Even if a parent could anticipate all these questions, a child is not sophisticated or clever enough to remember all the answers. As in the case I mentioned above, parents often initiate false allegations to ensure that an ex-partner does not get custody of the children. But this is like playing with fire because if the courts find that the allegations were false, they are willing to take placement away from the parent who made them and place a child with the falsely accused parent.

Children are put in the middle in instances of false allegations. When you involve your child in such a lie, he or she becomes a coconspirator. In foisting this role on your child, you are making him or her a victim of your actions and affecting his or her security needs and moral and ethical development.

In cases where a parent is guilty of sexual abuse, therapy usually elicits some kind of apology to the child. In only 10 percent of these cases do the offenders admit to what they did, so a parent often gives a generic apology, saying something like, "I want you to know that I'm really sorry for anything I did to hurt you." From that point on, the relationship can be carefully rebuilt. If history is then established between the child and parent that is different from the abusive past, the child will start trusting the parent more, feel good about him or her, and enjoy spending time together, even if it is supervised for some time.

If, however, a parent is guilty of sexual abuse and continues to insist that the child is lying, saying things such as, "How can you make up those horrible stories?" or "It's hard for me to love you when you say those kinds of things about me," the relationship will continue to deteriorate. In most of these cases, children still love that parent and, for them, one of the hardest parts of dealing with the abuse is knowing that it occurred and hearing the parent say it didn't. It's almost as if a child can forgive a parent for being sexually or physically abusive, but not for lying about it.

Apart from parents initiating false allegations against one another, other problems can be associated with charges of sexual abuse. As I said earlier, this type of abuse often occurs against children who are under the age of three and have not developed sufficient language skills to explain what has happened.

When very young children are involved, professionals sometimes have difficulty determining if abuse has occurred. I had a

154

case, for example, in which the father was accused of sexually abusing the daughter. He had requested visitation and as part of my evaluation, in consideration of that, I invited the child and both her parents to my office. He had not seen his daughter, who was then four years old, for about a year. I allowed the child to pick a seat in my office, which is very long and has 11 chairs, so she would feel that she had some control. She chose to sit closer to me. When her father came into the room, his daughter took one look at him and burst into tears. She wouldn't talk directly to him. She whispered questions to me and I repeated them to him.

When I conduct this type of evaluation, as part of this process, I ask children, "If you could ask your Daddy (Mommy) one question, what would it be?" and I ask parents the same thing, but their question is directed at the children. Well, this little girl asked her father, "Tell me about when I was a baby." That's a warm question. Children like their parents to tell them about the silly things they did when they were very little.

During this 20-minute observation, things warmed up and by the end there was no fearfulness on the child's part. When the father left the room and the mother came in to be briefed, before she even had a chance to sit down the little girl excitedly told her, "Guess what? I saw Daddy!" Her mother asked the child how the visit had been and the little girl walked to the chair where her father had been seated and patted it with her hand. It was still warm. She put her head down on the seat and rubbed her cheek against the warm spot.

In this case, I couldn't tell if abuse had occurred. It was clear to me that the child was still bonded to her father, and I suggested supervised contacts, moving to unsupervised contacts.

In another case, a family court ordered visitation for a mother who had been accused of sexually abusing her child after a court-appointed psychologist found no evidence of abuse. Her ex-spouse, who had custody of the child, complained about the visitation order and I was asked to do a second opinion evaluation with the child, who was five years old. The child provided a host of descriptions that made it clear that he had been sexually abused by his mother. I found that many crucial details had been ignored in the first evaluation and suggested that her visits be supervised.

The court changed the order so that the mother's visits were supervised.

I am convinced that for children in this two- to five-year age range, many genuine sexual abuse cases are not being pursued because the information is too gray, and a lot of physical abuse cases are being pursued as sexual abuse cases because the information is also too gray and people aren't sure what children are describing.

In most states, several different courts may hear sexual abuse cases. The criminal court hears cases when charges have been filed against someone by a district attorney. Family court hears sexual abuse cases containing an issue about visitation or placement being given to the alleged offender. Children's court may hear a case when it involves protective placement or protective orders. It is also possible for a case to be heard in all three courts at the same time.

In a family court setting, because the standard is "best interest of the child" and not "reasonable doubt" as it would be in criminal court, family court judges can deal with sexual abuse allegations that have been rejected by criminal courts. It is not uncommon, however, at the end of such a case for a family court judge to be unable to determine with certainty if the abuse occurred. Most judges are willing to err on the side of protecting a child. For example, a court may order supervised visitation for the accused parent even though there was no finding of sexual abuse in that case. Supervised visitation in a situation like this serves two purposes: it protects the child from the possibility of further sexual abuse and if the abuse did not occur, it protects the accused parent from further false allegations.

Psychological Effects of Sexual Abuse

A number of symptoms are manifested in children who have been sexually abused. One research review written in 1993, for example, showed that 38 percent of such children become sexually promiscuous, 35 percent have poor self-esteem, 37 percent have general behavior disorders, and 32 percent suffer post-traumatic stress disorder. The review concluded that children who had been molested frequently by someone close to them over a long period of time, in a manner that included force and oral, anal, or vaginal penetration, had a greater number of symptoms. Lack of a mother's support at the time the abuse was revealed (many mothers go into denial, especially if a spouse, relative, or boyfriend is accused) and a victim's negative outlook or coping style also increased symptoms. Not all children display symptoms. Some show symptoms that lessen over time, and others develop symptoms that worsen with time.

The more abusive an environment is, the more adversely it affects children. When you factor in the divorce process, knowing how it adversely affects all children, you are compounding the level and intensity of the problems.

Regardless of the degree to which they physically display a reaction to sexual abuse, all children are traumatized by abuse and allegations of it and what follows, which is having to testify in an open courtroom with the accused offender present throughout the proceeding. A child deals more effectively with the trauma of the event if closed circuit television or conferences in a judge's chambers can be substituted for testimony in an open court. Another component of court-related trauma is that it keeps the abuse alive in a child's mind and delays resolution. Adding to the difficulty of a court case is that it can take so long for a trial to begin that children may forget details, repress details, or become uncooperative.

False Memory Syndrome

The concept of False Memory Syndrome, or repressed and recovered memories (memories of traumatic events that suddenly come back to you after you've had no conscious memory of them), is very controversial because professionals argue that people are extremely vulnerable to the power of suggestion (their own and others'). Because of the recovered memories of others, people have admitted to acts they did not commit. Other people have been jailed based on recovered memories.

157

Although it is possible for someone to recover memories of events that occurred when he or she was younger, people can also fabricate stories, inaccurately recall incidents, or falsely "recall" things that never happened. Be wary of any professional who claims that all sexual abuse memories are false, or that all recovered memories are accurate.

Removal Cases

Although abuse constitutes a major area of concern in custody disputes, it is not the only problem that can arise. Imagine, for example, that you have been divorced for four years and except for some minor glitches, the placement schedule developed by you and your ex-spouse has worked well. Then, all of a sudden, you receive a phone call, letter, or formal notice that your ex-partner is moving out of town and wants to take the children along.

Let's assume that this move is for a legitimate purpose, such as a job transfer. What should you do? Should you fight the move? Let them go?

Whenever a move like this takes place, the children lose. A child who has had reasonable access to both parents and suddenly finds himself or herself in a position in which the other parent is going to be almost entirely excluded from his or her life is not going to be a happy child.

If an issue like this is taken to court, a judge will decide if the children move or stay. An ensuing court battle will be financially and psychologically costly, and the court will take a dim view of the parent who wants to move away with no real necessity. It becomes more difficult to convince the court that a child should move away when he or she will be leaving not only friends but extended family on both sides, a school in which he or she is performing adequately, and a neighborhood in which the child has enjoyed some stability. In such situations, the court is likely to allow children to remain behind with the nonmoving parent. In circumstances in which a move is essential and both you and your ex-spouse are excellent parents, the judge has a tough call to make, and very often small details—such as a child being able to have a pet in a new location or having to give one up—lead to a decision.

Several factors should be considered when you are deciding to take this issue to court. The first is whether the parent who is moving away will continue to allow you reasonable access to your children or if he or she will use the move to cut off your relationship. In situations that have been characterized by a lot of anger, lack of cooperation, difficulty obtaining compliance with court orders, and so on, your ex-spouse will more likely use moving away as an opportunity to cut you off from the children. And generally once the move is made, even if things do not go well, you will have difficulty getting the children back.

A second area that you need to evaluate is whether you can afford ongoing access. A court may order that you be allowed to visit your children, but suppose you can't afford it or you can't get the time off from work?

You also need to take into account the financial and psychological cost of fighting the move. Tens of thousands of dollars could be spent waging this battle over the course of a year or two, and that's money that could be used to visit your children in the other city. Psychologically, a court battle at this juncture could take a relationship that has been relatively cooperative and turn it topsy-turvy, and you are not likely to achieve the same level of cooperation afterwards.

This situation takes on another dimension when the move is being orchestrated for a marriage or new relationship. How does this affect children? To answer that question, I'll tell you about Tammy, who wanted to move from Wisconsin to Colorado with her children to marry a man she had known for three months. Her ex-husband was concerned about the planned move and went to court. In the interim, the guardian ad litem ordered a background check on the new significant other and found that he had an arrest record that included 17 convictions and a number of prison terms over ten years. The convictions included 2 for felonious armed robbery and 2 for felonious sexual assault.

The court ordered that Tammy could move to Colorado but the children were not to have contact with that man. In the ruling,

Tammy was also told that if she intended to marry him, she would not receive placement and her children would not be allowed to move with her.

What kind of influence would Tammy's new man have had on her children? Whose best interests was she looking after? What would have happened if her ex-husband had not intervened and the guardian ad litem had not stepped in to help resolve the matter? You must do your homework, be alert, and not let anything adversely affect your children. If you decide to allow your children to move with your ex-spouse, make sure a court order is entered or an agreement is signed allowing you significant access during nonschool time, similar to schedules outlined in Chapter 5.

Going Back to Court

People who need to return to court after a divorce are said to be dealing with "post judgment" concerns, meaning additional action is taking place after the original divorce judgment was entered.

One of the main reasons people return to court is because of a change of circumstance between the time a divorce was filed and the time they go to court to argue their case. A change of circumstance may include:

- A change in physical or mental health of a parent that reduces his or her capacity for carrying out parental abilities;
- A change in financial circumstances that makes it less feasible to adequately care for a child;
- Introduction of a new person into the children's lives who may be a negative influence (such as Tammy's significant other);
- Discovery of physical or sexual abuse;
- Repeated instances of bad judgment, such as sleeping with school-age children, taking children to bars, showing them R- or X-rated movies, or giving them illegal drugs;
- The onset of or return to alcohol or other drug abuse;

- An attempt to alienate the other parent;
- Lack of cooperation with court orders;
- Obstructing visits.

Change of circumstance can also involve one parent relocating and wanting to take the children with him or her. The presumption of the court is that children are better off when they don't have to change their residence, so, once again, the parent who is attempting to change must prove the necessity. In cases where the relocation seems unnecessary, the court is not likely to even entertain the notion. If a child's environment is not ideal, a parent may need to relocate to improve the child's living conditions. In such a case, the positive reason for the move would outweigh the negative impact on a child who has to change settings.

If a court battle ensues over a change of circumstance, it is likely that psychologists, social workers, and other professionals will be brought in to look into the concerns generated by the change or proposed change. As in all other instances, you must carefully weigh the financial and psychological cost of going back to court along with the cost of not fighting.

Contempt of Court

A judge can find you in contempt of court for not following his or her orders. It is unlikely, unless the infraction is extremely serious, that you would be found in contempt the first time you violate a court order. However, if more violations occur, a judge is likely to find you in contempt and give you a fine, jail time, or rescind your visitation privileges.

One of the most common reasons for finding a parent in contempt is failure to pay child support. Many parents have been jailed for this. Removing a child from the state without notifying the other parent can also result in a contempt finding or more serious findings.

Appeals

Television and movies have led us to believe that every court decision that someone doesn't like is appealed. In reality, very few divorce cases are appealed. When an appeal is filed, the appellate court is likely to refer the case back to the court and judge who made the original decision and ask him or her to reconsider it. In most cases, when an appeal is made, the appellate court up-holds the original decision. This doesn't mean that you should not appeal a decision with which you are dissatisfied. It just means that you have to consider the circumstances, what you and your children stand to gain or lose, and the financial and psychological costs of appealing a case. Generally, psychological wounds created by the divorce will remain open during the appeal process, pro-longing your recovery and that of your children.

Child Support

The sole purpose of child support is to support your children. It should not be used to redecorate the home, take vacations, or for other inappropriate things. Child support consistently misused can represent a change of circumstance and a judge might con-sider changing placement of the children.

Most states have guidelines or laws to accurately determine how much money is needed to support a child. Support should be ordered on a percentage of income basis instead of a dollar amount because as the cost of living increases, the dollar amount may be insufficient. Some states have support payments automat-ically deducted from the paying parent's payroll check. The money is sent to the court, which then sends it to the primary placement parent. If the person paying support loses his or her job, support payments are likely to be temporarily suspended.

Kidnapping

You may entertain the fantasy of running away with your children if divorce and custody battles become really bad. Just be sober about this and remember that it's a terrible idea. In the vast ma-jority of parental kidnapping cases, the parent is located and many are convicted of the crime and jailed. Apart from the criminal implications and ramifications, if you take your children and you are found, you will probably never be able to spend unsupervised time with them again. To compound matters, the very person you are trying to keep your children from will probably be awarded placement while you are in jail and, most likely, permanently.

Parents sometimes think they can flee to a foreign country where they will never be found. This is not true. Any country that belongs to the Hague Convention will help find children and will return them to the country from which they were taken. Depending on the laws of the country in which the children are found, the parent who absconded with them will either be jailed there or returned to the country from which the children were snatched. Many countries have kidnapping laws that are stricter than those in the United States.

The Hague Convention

The Hague Convention was adopted for a number of reasons, not the least of which was to deal with the difficulty of locating children in foreign countries. It also serves to facilitate problems locating attorneys in countries to where a child has been abducted and to reduce difficulty having a custody order recognized in a foreign country. In the past, parents who abducted their children would often go to court in a foreign country to get a court order for their custody, thereby legitimizing the abduction. The situation would contain two conflicting court orders, which made it even more difficult to have children returned home.

The Hague Convention attempts to facilitate the prompt return of children to the country from which they were kidnapped and to ensure the custody rights and laws of that country. Under the Convention, a judge must order the return of children under the age of 16 when they have been wrongfully taken from a country. Exceptions allowed for not returning children under the Convention include a great risk of physical or psychological harm, an objection by the child to being returned when he or she is old enough to make that objection, or a violation of human rights principles if the child were returned.

163

As of 1994, countries subscribing to the Hague Convention included Argentina, Australia, Austria, Bahamas, Belize, Bosnia and Herzegovina, Burkina Faso, Canada, Croatia, Denmark, Ecuador, France, Germany, Greece, Hungary, Ireland, Israel, Luxembourg, Macedonia, Mauritius, Mexico, Monaco, Netherlands, New Zealand, Norway, Poland, Portugal, Romania, Spain, Sweden, Switzerland, United Kingdom, and United States. If a child is removed from the country by your former spouse, notify your attorney immediately.

▼
Chapter

8

The Only Certainty in Life Is Change

One of the toughest elements of divorce is that life can change literally overnight and keep on changing, sometimes with little forewarning. The instability and upheaval this brings keeps everyone off balance and in a constant state of confusion and anxiety. This is troublesome, at best, for adults, but it is completely disconcerting for children.

Removal cases are a classic example of the kind of rapid and dramatic change that can occur in divorce and custody situations. In many respects, removals are more difficult than any other cases related to custody because they are often precipitated by average lifestyle changes over which you may have no control. If a company relocates to another city, you may have to follow your job, or if you lose your job or change careers, you may have to relocate to find suitable employment.

When children are a consideration, relocation can be extraordinarily trying, particularly if the children have been able to settle into a comfortable routine without major flare-ups between you and your ex-spouse. When one of you has to leave suddenly, your children are once again confronted with feelings of abandonment, helplessness, and fear of loss.

If a loving relationship exists between children and both parents, it is only natural for the parent who is leaving to want the children to make the move too. This is especially true of parents who don't have primary placement. It's also normal for a parent to ask the children if moving is something they would like to do. On the other side, the parent who is staying behind doesn't want the children to leave. Unfortunately, this situation puts children back into the undesirable position of choosing between their parents, and also revives those unsettling questions about where they are going to live and with whom and where they are going to go to school; that is, where they are going to grow up.

Clearly, children can't live in two places at once. So, if you've had a situation that was working relatively well and through no one's fault the system has to be dismantled, one parent is going to end up the winner and one will be the loser, who will ultimately be relegated to the position of visitor. The losing parent must also deal with the fear that his or her good relationship with the children is going to be jeopardized and may even deteriorate.

Everyone involved must deal with feelings of loss and anger, and the parent on the losing side may also confront the grief cycle again. Children are even more upset in this situation because their parents are upset.

Typically, if the primary placement parent intends to move out of state with the children, he or she must file a formal notice to the other parent. Don't succumb to any temptation to just make the move, figuring that once it's done no one will reverse it. You can't move in the middle of the night without anyone knowing because if you do, you will be ordered back by the courts until the matter can be sorted out. And think of what this kind of surreptitious action will do to your children. This takes us back to the issue of secrecy and the burden it places on them. Children will be frightened, worried, and in total turmoil. They will worry about the other parent's feelings and actions, and may ask you such things as, "What will happen when Mom finds out?" or "Is Daddy going to be mad about this?" or "Is Daddy going to be sad when he finds out we're gone?" These concerns are compounded if you decide to move without your ex-partner's knowledge and consent and if you lie to the children, telling them they are going on vacation or that you're only going to stay in the new location for a short time.

What often happens in relocation situations is that the ugliness that parents may have been able to avoid by having worked out acceptable placement and visitation schedules suddenly surfaces. The custody dispute is resurrected and parents engage in pettiness while trying to prove who is best suited to have the children.

People point to minor incidents or negligible visitation infractions, leaving each other saying, "I can't believe you're bringing that up. I never knew that was an issue," or "That was never a problem before." They mention incidents such as a spanking that occurred years before or a time when Dad's girlfriend didn't leave before the children arrived for a visit or a time when Mom didn't tell the baby-sitter to come at a particular hour and the children were home alone for a while. Little mistakes that are generally overlooked for the sake of peace now become issues. Whereas previously you were able to avoid this kind of acrimony and your children became accustomed to a manageable truce between the two of you, now your children see their parents shooting barbs at each other, and they think, "Where did these monsters come from?"

When news of a planned relocation is first presented to the children, the person telling them may not think that a custody dispute will ensue, especially if the two ex-partners have found a way to work together for the children. If the primary placement parent is moving, he or she may figure that primary placement allows for the children to simply make the move. The parent doesn't recognize that the other parent has the right to object.

A case involving four children whose mother decided to move to Arizona heated up when she wanted to take the children with her. The court said that she had no pressing reason to move and that the children should stay in the state in which they were living. After her ex-husband was given placement, she turned on the children, and went so far as to lock them out of her home at Christmastime, denying them access to money they had saved to buy gifts, presents they had already purchased, and all their belongings.

Parents who allow this type of situation to escalate to such dramatic and hurtful proportions are sometimes blaming their children for the court's decision, accusing them of being in cahoots with the other parent and choosing sides. Children can't understand why this happens. If one parent tries to be soothing by giving the children too much information about what's going on, they become even more confused, upset, and directly involved in adult issues. If the other parent does spiteful, destructive things, such as locking the children out at Christmastime, the children eventually become angry with that parent and the relationship grows more strained. Some children move to a position where they don't even want to see the other parent, because of anger or fear of further hurtful actions or because they need to protect themselves emotionally and/or physically.

Longer Lasting Reactions

In a general mental health sense, if something that has caused an individual to suffer emotionally happens a second time, the emotional reaction will usually recur faster and it will be deeper and last longer. This principle can be applied to divorce situations. If children who came through a difficult divorce and for whom life finally regained some semblance of normalcy suddenly learn that they have to go through it all over again because of a dispute involving a move, whatever problems they initially experienced will happen faster, will happen with greater intensity, and will last longer. This reaction also applies to adults.

Parents who may have dealt well with their children's emotional problems when the divorce originally occurred may now find themselves dealing with children who are older and whose emotional problems take on characteristics specific to their age group (as mentioned in Chapter 2), and those problems have to be dealt with differently. For example, a child who was six when your divorce originally occurred would have been at an egocentric stage in which the child believed everything was his or her fault and all your energy would have gone into explaining that the child wasn't to blame. If a custody dispute occurs five years later, for example, when the child is 11, he or she is in the middle of the age of anger and you will see a completely different reaction. Your child may say, "You can't do this to me. I'm going to go live with my friends," or "I'm going to run away." A teenager may say, "You've already screwed up my life once. You're not going to do it again."

Another factor that may arise in custody disputes erupting several years after a divorce is that one parent may have remarried and have children through that marriage. It's not uncommon in such situations for the parent who is going to be left without the children in common to say to the remarried parent: "You have other children now. Why can't you give up the ones we had together?" If the other parent loves the children, he or she is going to be unwilling to do that.

A Plan to Make Everyone Feel Better

Don't put your children into any of these positions, especially if you have taken the matter to court, because the court is where the decision is going to be made.

As I said before, when a relocation dispute erupts, one of the first things authorities do is try to determine the necessity of the move. If it looks as if someone is doing it for superficial reasons or to get away from the other parent, the court is likely to say that the parent who wants to move can do so, but the children must stay behind. Remember, courts are generally inclined to leave the children where they are barring any major problems. Very often, when such a ruling is made, the parent doesn't leave.

Sometimes when a move is justified, primary placement may be determined by little details, such as one parent may smoke and the child has asthma, or one parent has a pet to which the child is allergic, or one parent tells the children too much about adult issues such as court proceedings or financial arrangements. If a job is at issue, authorities look to see if a similar job could have been found that would have made the move unnecessary.

Neither of you are to be blamed for the feelings you experience at a time like this, but you can't allow the situation to be controlled by your emotions. Once again, you must think of the best interests of your children. The best approach is to try to work this out to everyone's satisfaction, using visitation schedules that have already been discussed through which both of you can see the children as much as possible.

Many parents agree to this type of scheduling as a way of feeling better about letting children relocate. Even if you don't exercise the visitation plan you choose to its fullest, you will at least have the reassurance of knowing that it's in place and that you can have meaningful contact with your children throughout the year.

The Challenge of Additional Adjustments

All forms of change require an adjustment period, but removals or relocations require additional adjustment time. The most stressful things that can occur in people's lives are marriage, divorce, death of a loved one, loss of or changing a job, and moving. In removal situations, four of those major stressors may be operating simultaneously—the move, the divorce, perhaps marriage if that is the reason for the relocation, and changing jobs.

When you place children in this type of situation, they not only have to recover from the acrimony of the custody dispute, they must also adjust to the move, a new school, new home, and new friends, as well as to the parent who is dealing with these major stressors. This adjustment can take a considerable amount of time, so be patient with yourself and your children. Deal with age-specific problems as they arise and, if necessary, get therapy for everyone involved.

Just When You Thought You Had Enough to Deal With

While all this is unfolding, you may also be grappling with establishing new relationships. Although you may feel at the time of divorce that you have no desire to get involved in another relationship, or that you have little likelihood of doing so, don't discount the possibility of a new relationship.

It is not unusual for dating to start during separation or shortly after divorce. It is also not unusual to be involved in one or more transitional relationships. A transitional relationship is usually short-lived and helps one or both individuals get through a transitional period in life. You may be attracted to someone who has characteristics that your ex-spouse was lacking and you immediately feel an affinity for this person. You may even feel that he or she is the only one for you in the world, but be careful. Rushing into transitional relationships and trying to make them permanent can be detrimental to you and your children.

When you start dating, remember the magical wish your children carry with them that you and your ex-spouse will be reunited. This wish may be strong enough for your children to actively or unconsciously try to sabotage your new relationships. Obviously, if you remarry, your children's fantasy will be dashed, so they perceive that it is in their best interests if you don't remarry.

You may begin by dating a number of individuals, and from your vantage point, this approach has nothing wrong with it. However, your children should not be introduced to every new person you date. They need some stability at this time in their lives, and being introduced to people who may be in their lives for a short time does not contribute to stability. You are best off not introducing children to someone you are dating until you have seen him or her for a long time and the relationship has a serious element to it.

Also consider that children may still have open wounds from your divorce. If you introduce a new man or woman into their lives too suddenly, they may feel as though you are trying to replace their other parent. Your children may resent this, thinking, "I don't want you pretending that you're happy with this new friend when I'm unhappy that you and Mom (Dad) aren't living together."

Too often parents try to push this too fast as a way of compensating to the children for the loss of the marital relationship, but what they're more than likely to do is turn the children off to the new partner. If you add to this the element that you may have a different friend every few weeks, it gets to the point where children become disgusted and say, "Don't drag me through all of this until you've made up your mind." And all the while they are inwardly holding onto their magical wish. Another danger associated with introducing children to every new partner you meet is that if you end up in a custody dispute, the guardian ad litem or judge may ask how you have demonstrated stability when you have subjected your children to one partner after another.

Introduce children to a new partner gradually. The first time your children meet him or her should not be on a week-long trip to Walt Disney World. The initial few contacts should be brief and informal. A formal dinner at a restaurant, for example, may seem appropriate, but it will put a lot of pressure on everyone and may overpower children. Such a meal can be costly, requires everyone to dress up, and carries expectations that good things will result when the outcome may be the exact opposite.

Doing simple things that your children are interested in will increase their comfort level. For example, you might want to take them and this new person for an ice cream cone, or you could visit your new partner's home for 15 to 30 minutes, just to drop something off or to introduce your children to his or her children, if that is the case. In so doing, your children will have a visual image of what this person looks like, but you won't be putting them in a position where they have to establish a relationship. To heighten comfort even further, if your new friend has a pet it should be present when you make your introductions.

After you've done two or three informal things, you can plan something more elaborate, such as a dinner. Taking your children and new friend to see a movie is a good idea because no one has to talk or interact except while traveling to and from the theater.

Wait even longer to display affection toward your new friend in front of your children because they may be accustomed to seeing only their parents act that way and think that is what affection between adults is reserved for. As early as possible, your new partner or you should explain that he or she is not in your life to replace the other parent. Let your friend explain, "I'm just a new person in your life," and tell the children what to call him or her.

172

Decide what message you want to send the first time your new partner stays overnight and your children know it. If you don't have a problem with your children being aware of the concept of sexual activity outside a marital relationship, you should have no concern about sharing a bed with your new partner with your children present in your home. However, if you don't want your children being exposed to this type of situation, don't have your partner sleep over, or have one of you sleep on the sofa or in a guest room. I remind you once again that children learn what they live. If this is the behavior to which they are exposed, you can't complain when your 19-year-old decides to live with a boyfriend or girlfriend. You can't hold them to a double standard that says such behavior is all right for you but not for them.

Letting your children get to know your friends should be progressive and so should introducing the concept of an overnight stay. Keep in mind your ideas of what you expose your children to and how soon. The overnight stay should not occur until children know this new person well and have spent considerable time with him or her. Remain mindful of your children's feelings, which should take precedence over your own.

I was involved with a case in which the mother brought her four-year-old son to his father's for a visit and they found the father and his girlfriend in bed. This wasn't a situation in which the friend was staying over in the presence of the child; she just didn't leave fast enough. The little boy was extremely upset because this was the marital bed and he was accustomed to seeing his mother and father in it together.

Parents often say they don't want their children exposed to an ex-spouse sleeping with someone, claiming this is immoral, religiously inappropriate, or improper. Not all people embrace those beliefs and you can't hold others to your standards. I recall a judge once telling a mother, "Ma'am, you may not like your children being exposed to your ex-husband living with his girlfriend out of wedlock, but it is more important for your children to see a loving relationship between two adults, considering the fighting between you and your former husband, than worrying about whether they are living together out of wedlock."

Remarriage

If you decide to remarry, how are you going to execute your plans? Some people decide to get married without telling family members, including their children. Although you may think this is romantic, or a way of avoiding outside objections and influences, such an action undermines children's sense of security and whatever trust they have in you as a parent.

Whenever possible, include children in your marriage ceremony. Do not, I repeat, do not forbid your children to attend your ex-spouse's marriage. Parents have actually stopped children from sharing in an ex-partner's joy because the wedding occurred during their placement time! Behavior like this only generates an enormous amount of anger and resentment in your ex-partner and your children.

Here are other things to keep in mind before you remarry:

- Whose house will you live in?
- Where will the children stay?
- Will there be room for your children in your new home?
- If your new partner has children, who will be staying where?

As I said before, living arrangements are a big issue for children. I am reminded of a girl who told me that each of her parents had "six children." Including herself, there were actually seven brothers and sisters. Five of these children were common to the mother and father and each parent had an additional child from a new relationship. How you handle this type of situation will have a lot of bearing on how your children react and adjust to a new marriage and new siblings.

All These Children

When parents remarry and have additional children, the family will include natural brothers and sisters, stepbrothers and stepsisters, and half brothers and half sisters. Stepbrothers and stepsisters have neither parent in common. Half brothers and half sisters share a mother or a father.

174

Visitation schedules in extended families can be downright confusing for everyone, especially children. Assume, for example, that Mom has two children from a previous marriage, Dad has two children from a previous marriage, and Mom and Dad have two children from a current marriage. The four children from previous marriages will spend time in two households. However, are visitation schedules arranged so that all six children spend time together?

Visitation and living arrangements should be resolved before marriage. As a general rule, try to have all the children together for some periods of time. Consequently, you must consider if you will have room in your new household to accommodate all the children at one time and to make them feel comfortable in both homes.

Until scheduling becomes automatic, your life can feel like a quest for day-to-day survival as you wonder who is going to be at your home on any given day of the week, how many people you will have to feed, how much laundry will have to be done, and who has to be picked up and where. No matter how traumatic it seems at the outset, the situation will become automatic if you work with a good master schedule that is accessible to everyone. When establishing a visitation schedule, keep in mind that the fewer transitions you build into it, the easier it's going to be for you and the children to understand and remember.

You won't need to worry about introductions if you and all the children have spent time together before the marriage at zoos, ball games, playgrounds, and so on. You will, however, need to concern yourself with other day-to-day issues, such as who will discipline the children, who will arrange schedules, and who will set rules. Such issues can be volatile and blow up very quickly, so they should not be ignored or relegated to the position of secondary concerns.

You also need to consider sibling rivalry and natural birth order. For example, a child who was the oldest or youngest in the family may no longer hold that position after you remarry. Parents often overlook the adjustment that this repositioning involves. Be advised that there is no easy way to deal with it. Patience, understanding, and communication are crucial but sometimes not enough, and you should not hesitate to seek professional guidance. More and more organizations sponsor support and therapy groups for blended families (as this type of extended family is called), and you may want to take advantage of them.

The Role of the Stepparent

Sensitive issues don't end with figuring out a way to blend and schedule your extended family. One of the most ticklish issues is deciding what to call the stepparent. More hard feelings are created and more time is wasted in court with arguments over one parent allowing his or her children to call a stepparent Mom or Dad than could be imagined.

I don't advise the use of the label *Mom* or *Dad* for stepparents. Your new partner can be called by his or her first name or Stepmom or Stepdad. Allowing a child to call your new partner Mom or Dad suggests that he or she is replacing the natural parent. It is particularly detrimental if a parent instructs a child to call his or her new partner Mom or Dad and to not refer to the natural parent that way but instead use his or her first name. Such instructions are given in order to undermine a parent's role and to reduce his or her importance in a child's life. Courts have been known to transfer placement of children over this issue.

This situation is very confusing and hurtful for children. I had a case in which a five-year-old boy had a natural mother, a former stepmother, and a new stepmother. His father insisted that the child call each of them Mom. This child's solution to reducing his confusion was to call one Mommy, one Mamma, and the other Mommer.

If, however, your children do call your ex-spouse's new partner Mom or Dad, don't assume that they have been instructed to do so. Some children do this on their own, and your ex-spouse has the responsibility of asking the children to discontinue it. If this happens, make your ex-spouse aware of it. He or she will need to explain, once again, that this new partner has not taken the place of a natural parent, and that the term *Mom* or *Dad* is reserved for one's birth parent.

Disciplining Children

A stepparent's role in disciplining children needs to be carefully considered and defined. You and your new partner should start by discussing your ideas on what discipline entails, how it will be carried out, and by whom. Resolve any differences at the outset of your marriage. A number of disciplinary measures that do not involve physical punishment can be used with children, such as time-outs or loss of privileges. Some parents, however, still use forms of physical punishment, such as spankings. Punishments that you rarely or never employed when dealing with your child should not become a norm because your new partner advocates them.

Spanking is not an appropriate form of discipline. Any form of physical punishment has negative side effects. Children who are spanked or subjected to physical punishment learn that when you are frustrated, you hit. Through the use of physical punishment, children learn to avoid the punisher rather than the act for which they were punished, they learn how to escape from the punishment situation, and they engage in behavior that is referred to as counteraggression, in which they strike back at the hitter or someone else.

A more difficult situation arises when your ex-spouse becomes upset when your new partner disciplines his or her children. Some households clearly decide that only the natural parent will discipline the children, especially if spanking is used as a punishment. Although this decision may theoretically resolve concerns about who metes out discipline, parents will find it imprudent at times to reserve discipline for only a natural parent. For example, if a natural parent is out of town and discipline is necessary, the stepparent is foolish to say, "Wait until your father gets home in three days. He'll punish you for this." By the time discipline is finally implemented, a child has already moved on to other issues and the discipline may no longer be relevant. Waiting is appropriate if a child has committed a major infraction that requires some negotiating to determine proper discipline.

If you and your ex-spouse clash about your new partner disciplining your children, all adults concerned should meet to dis-

177

cuss this and find common ground. The last thing you want is for parents and stepparents to be implementing many different types of discipline. Such a situation allows children to manipulate parents and stepparents, to get away with negative behavior, and to undermine parental judgment.

Cementing Relationships

As difficult as some of these issues may be for stepparents, they can take steps to assume a special role. One is to serve as a facilitator, fostering positive relationships between children and their natural parents. As I've said, children should be encouraged to maintain their relationship with the other parent, and to remember holidays, birthdays, and other special occasions. A stepparent can help children select gifts and cards or plan special things for their natural parents.

A stepparent can also serve as a moderating influence when difficulties arise between natural parents. Either or both natural parents can at times lose their perspective, exercising poor judgment, becoming unnecessarily angry, or distancing themselves from a situation. Since a stepparent is a trusted partner, he or she can provide a voice of reason and more objective, meaningful feedback, helping a parent realize that what he or she was doing was inappropriate.

Stepparents, however, can knowingly or unknowingly tip the balance of a relationship between the natural parents in an unfavorable direction. A stepparent may become jealous and devisive about children's relationships with their natural parents or encourage a partner to become competitive over visitation time. This can lead to harsh feelings among a parent, an ex-spouse, and a stepparent. Situations like this are best resolved by having all parties meet in an informal or formal setting, such as a therapeutic environment.

The Other Extended Family

Other family members, such as grandparents, aunts, uncles, and cousins, can also be helpful in smoothing the rough edges of a blended family. Children and adults need to continue relationships with these extended family members after divorce and remarriage. Extended family members should be allowed to continue having a relationship with both sets of parents and the children.

If you have remarried and now have three or four sets of extended family members, time and location constraints may make it impossible for children to have meaningful relationships with all of them. When conflicts arise, relationships with natural parents' extended families should take precedence over relationships with stepparents' extended families.

Change as Children Grow Older

Even after you remarry and deal with all the issues that need to be addressed, as long as your children are children, change will continue. No court order or mediation agreement can successfully be made that will apply to an entire childhood. Changes occur as children get older and parents need to be flexible and understanding.

Very young children need your time and attention with developmental and learning skills. Children in their middle school years have additional needs as they start becoming involved in Little League sports, dance classes, and other outside activities. It is inevitable that some of these events will interfere with placement and visitation schedules. If your visiting time is changed because of activity schedules, don't misinterpret that as sabotage by the other parent. Parents must be flexible to accommodate activities because these activities can be crucial to your child's good health and proper development. However, if activity schedules constantly interfere with placement, sacrifices will have to be made. Either some activities will have to be eliminated or the parent who is missing visiting time should have the children during these activities and be responsible for transporting them to and from the activities.

Other issues arise when children reach their teenage years. Remember, a teenager's job is to separate and individuate from

179

parents. They may be involved in school plays, clubs, or athletics. When both my children were in high school, the four of us rarely sat at the table together for dinner more than once or twice a week. We were just not able to mesh everybody's schedules, considering practice times, meetings, and work hours. The same concerns affect regular placement schedules in divorce situations.

It is not unusual for children to reach their high school years and not want to adhere to alternate weekend placement. This behavior is not rejection by them or interference by the other parent, but is evidence that the children no longer want to spend a whole weekend with a parent. Look at this as a sign of maturation and growth. Once your children reach their teenage years, they don't need to see you as often to maintain an adequate and satisfying relationship with you or to continue the psychological bond you share. After all, children who attend boarding schools, camps, and college maintain a relationship with their parents. Don't feel threatened by your child's natural growth—enjoy it.

180

▼
Chapter
9

Custody Do's and Don'ts

We love our children and should enjoy them, and yet we often contribute to their trials and sometimes their destruction. Each of us pulls an imaginary little red cart behind us, filled with emotional baggage that we collect along life's way. As parents, we heap (sometimes unwittingly and sometimes knowingly) a lot of cargo into our children's red carts, which they have to unload at some point or be left pulling around for the rest of their lives.

To illustrate the negative impact you can have on your children when problems are not promptly and adequately resolved, I am recounting a case from my files involving a boy named Chris. Not every child whose parents divorce and cannot communicate with one another ends up as badly as Chris. However, even this worst case scenario could happen in your family. While reading this chapter, think about the many situations that have been discussed in this book and note how many of them occurred in this case.

A Boy Named Chris

I met Chris and his parents for the first time in February 1993. They came to see me because of behavior problems they were noticing in Chris and his brother, Larry. Psychological testing was done on Chris and I found that the depressionlike symptoms he was exhibiting were directly related to the ongoing fighting between his mother and father, even though they had been divorced for four and a half years.

Both parents had remarried, but neither had children from their second marriages. Chris's father, who had primary placement of the children, was a retired Army officer and his mother was a homemaker. Their arguing centered around the father's contention that his ex-wife was too lax and unstructured in all ways, including bringing up the children, and she believed that he was too rigid, controlling, and structured.

I told them about the negative effects that divorced parents arguing for five years can have on their children, but they seemed disbelieving. My primary concern was not doing individual therapy with Chris, but family therapy with the group, and I told his parents so. They agreed to begin therapy for themselves and then gradually introduce the boys to the sessions.

Brother Larry

After several sessions with Chris's parents, I began therapy with his brother, Larry. Not only did Larry also appear to be depressed, but he was stuttering severely and had been in speech and language therapy through school for some time. Larry's stuttering increased noticeably whenever he was under psychological stress, but during therapy, when he talked about his parents' arguments, his stuttering became so dramatic that sometimes he was not understandable. His stuttering also increased whenever he was around his parents.

After several months, the stuttering almost completely stopped during therapy. Mild stuttering returned only on occasion when Larry discussed problems with his parents.

182

Chris

Chris was a 14-year-old freshman in a public high school outside metropolitan Milwaukee when I met him. Early in therapy he told me that he was greatly distressed by the arguments between his parents. They shouted at each other whenever they met and over the phone, badgered each other incessantly, slammed and threw things, and carried on over the same issues constantly. Every time Chris was with his father, the man continually bad-mouthed his ex-wife; whenever Chris was with his mother, she spent the time in constant criticism of Chris's father. Chris was so distraught over the situation with his parents that he was reduced to tears several times in my office while witnessing them argue over minor differences.

In September 1993, Chris's father called me to say that he had taken the boy to a hospital emergency room because he thought Chris was having seizures. Chris had been unable to recall portions of what had occurred over the weekend with his father, describing himself as having "lost all memory."

Doctors performed a number of tests on Chris, including a brain wave test, to be sure he hadn't suffered any seizures. All the tests were negative. They decided that Chris had had an acute psychotic episode. (Psychosis is a state of mind during which an individual is unable to distinguish reality from fantasy. During psychotic episodes, people separate themselves from reality.)

I had Chris transferred to the adolescent unit of Charter Hospital, where it was determined during his admission interview that he was indeed psychotic. He was unable to identify himself, and didn't know where he was or what day it was. He was unable to identify his parents, and he didn't recognize me, even though we had worked together in therapy for eight months.

Several days later, I asked Chris if he could recall anything that occurred while he was being admitted to the hospital. He was only able to remember one thing from that time period—an argument between his mother and father over how old Chris had been when he had the measles. This answer was very revealing. There was Chris, in a psychotic state in front of his parents; their response was to argue about something inconsequential, and that's what he remembered.

During his first week in the hospital, Chris told me he had a large collection of knives and a gun hidden in his bedroom. Neither parent had been aware of this. He said he had to keep the weapons for protection against whomever was trying to kill him, although he couldn't be specific about who that was. This conversation was further evidence of the psychotic fantasy Chris was experiencing.

He was also having auditory and visual hallucinations, hearing and seeing things that were not real. Chris said he was hearing disembodied voices inside his head telling him, "I will kill you. You can't hide from me. Why don't you just kill yourself? Why don't you just kill your parents?" I was literally chilled by this.

Chris said that because of what the voices were saying, he had thought about killing himself, at one point cutting himself and scraping his wrists with knives from his collection, and had also considered killing his parents. Chris was given antipsychotic medication because these hallucinations were continuing.

Over time, the extremely fragile state of Chris's ego became apparent. Whenever Chris became more anxious, he slipped deeper into a psychotic episode. For example, one day his mother was supposed to bring a jacket to the hospital for him to wear. He was so convinced that she would not remember the garment that he cried uncontrollably during a group therapy session. He then wrapped himself into a fetal position and no one could communicate with him. A staff member went to Chris's room, found the jacket—which his mother had brought while he was with the group—and brought it to Chris, but it was hours before he was able to start pulling himself out of that episode.

It was not unusual for Chris to deny having the hallucinations or delusions two or three days after reporting them. These episodes were so frightening to him that he had to deny that they had occurred to protect himself from them. This alternation between a psychotic state and denial made this case very difficult to treat because unless Chris admitted that the problems existed, we couldn't start to deal with them effectively. Chris's denial of the psychotic events led his father to conclude that Chris had nothing wrong with him, and that he was acting psychotic because he wanted more attention from his mother.

Chris's parents continued arguing during family sessions at the hospital. He responded by curling up in a fetal position in a chair, rocking back and forth and sobbing. His parents ignored this regressive behavior and kept on arguing with one another. I told these people that if they didn't find a way to communicate more effectively with one another, they might permanently lose their child to psychosis or suicide, but they were unable to stop arguing. Chris's father said he recalled the warning I had given them in February about how seriously arguing could affect Chris, but he said he didn't believe it could happen to his child.

After each family session, Chris slipped back into seeing and hearing things, especially the voices telling him to kill himself or his parents. His ego simply wasn't strong enough to deal with what his parents were doing and it seemed to become more fragile every time he was exposed to them.

Chris had the maturity of a nine-year-old, and it was interesting to note that he was that age when his parents actually divorced. His entire psychological development had been arrested for five years while he used whatever psychic energy he had to deal with his parents' arguing instead of continuing his psychological development. Now, with Chris hospitalized, his mother began realizing that she and her ex-husband were responsible for his condition, but his father didn't heed these concerns and he blatantly continued the behavior that had so seriously impacted his son.

Chris was hospitalized for seven weeks, during which time he was discharged twice but came back to the hospital after a day or two because of severe regressive behavior. When he finally was able to leave the hospital, he was unable to return to school full-time. His ego was still so fragile that he couldn't take part in any activity that required consistent attention and focus.

Chris's father said he couldn't see that any good had come from his son's hospitalization, a response that was both sad and frightening. He criticized the hospital staff as being incompetent and was upset by a social worker who had continually confronted him about the impact his behavior was having on Chris. Instead of heeding the social worker, Chris's father blamed his ex-wife for all the hostility between them.

Chris's mother recognized how dangerous it was to let Chris continue living with his father, but his father would not voluntarily agree to a change of placement. This put Chris's mother in a lose-lose situation, forcing her to decide between leaving Chris with his father, and thereby subjecting him to further psychological damage, or going back to court. She was justifiably concerned that taking the matter to court could lead Chris to regress further and perhaps even cause permanent mental illness. She took a chance, went back to court, and won primary placement of Chris.

Why a Shattered Ego?

Why did this happen to Chris? To answer that, we must understand that the ego is that part of the personality that is the self-concept, or self identity, and that tries to obtain a balance between impulses and conscience. It was very difficult for Chris to gain a strong ego-identity by observing his parents. His mother was unstructured and described her home as chaotic at times, but she was also a caring woman who showed Chris a lot of love.

It was true that Chris's father was rigid and highly structured, and although he loved Chris very much, he had difficulty showing it. When Chris was with his mother, she described his father's approach to life as inappropriate, and when Chris was with his father, he described his mother the same way. As a result, Chris's already weakened ego couldn't find a firm foundation for the growth of his self-concept. Each time he tried to identify with one of his parents for a foundation on which to build his identity, the other parent would shatter and undermine the identity he was building.

Chris became so anxious and depressed about the ongoing fighting between his parents that he began thinking about killing himself to escape having to deal with them. His ego was under constant attack by their hostility toward each other. Eventually, Chris's ego couldn't handle these attacks anymore and it shattered. His mind then allowed itself to become psychotic to prevent Chris from committing suicide.

After Hospitalization

Chris experienced three regressive episodes in the week after he left the hospital, which caused him to be rehospitalized. Once, he became terrified that his mother was going to kill herself because she was so upset over his behavior, even though she never gave any indication that she was suicidal. Another time, he said he felt extremely unsafe in his father's house and had more suicidal thoughts.

His parents responded to this by blaming each other: his mother said she was going to court to get Chris away from his father before he destroyed the boy, and his father drew up a list of "facts" about what he considered to be proof of his ex-wife's incompetence.

Within one month of Chris's discharge from the hospital, his father stopped Chris's therapy, discontinued all his medication, and told him to stop his attention-getting behavior. He took control of Chris's life and began serving as Chris's ego.

Now, more than a year after his discharge, Chris lives with his mother on a full-time basis and rarely sees his father. The only way he was able to keep his ego intact enough so he could start building his way back was to separate himself psychologically from his father. Larry decided to live with his father, which added another sad component to the outcome of this situation because the two brothers seldom see each other.

I sometimes wonder what it takes for parents to understand the effects of their behavior on their children. In Chris's case, two relatively intelligent parents were unable to put their differences aside long enough to prevent their son from becoming psychotic. A number of major issues arose in Chris's case: the ongoing fighting between his parents, which negatively impacted the children; the questions about taking the case back to court; the overall negative impact of divorce on children; the parents' need to express anger taking precedence over love for their children; the impact of parental arguing on a child's social development; and change of placement.

As I have said throughout this book, you can do many things to make your divorce as reasonable as possible so that what hap-

187

pened to Chris doesn't happen to your children. I am giving you a list of do's and don'ts. The more do's you follow, the more likely you will be able to obtain custody or placement. The more don'ts you build into your life, the less likely a court will be to rule in your favor.

Custody Do's

1. Attempt mediation before litigation.

2. Understand from the outset that two parents living apart will not see their children as often as two parents living together.

3. Anticipate that two adults living apart will have more expenses than two adults living together.

4. Consider a joint custody arrangement rather than sole custody.

5. Be willing to share holidays rather than alternating them.

6. Be together (with your spouse) when you tell your children about your separation and/or divorce.

7. Provide stability; don't move from one home to another more often than necessary.

8. Be sensitive to your children's needs as well as your own.

9. Plan and consult with each other in advance of placement/visitation time with your children.

10. Observe time schedules with your children as strictly as possible.

11. Be flexible regarding visitation times for each parent.

12. Do whatever is necessary to resolve angry feelings toward your ex-spouse.

13. Refrain from giving your children too much decision-making power.

14. Tell your children often that they are still loved and that they are not getting divorced from their parents.

15. Give children therapeutic opportunities if their psychological adjustment appears to be too problematic.

16. Create an emotional environment for your children that allows them to continue to love and spend time with the other parent. Allow them to telephone on a reasonable basis.

17. Present a united front when handling problems with the children.

18. Encourage a good relationship between the children and the other parent's extended family.

19. Encourage children to remember the other parent on special occasions, allowing them to buy cards and gifts and to telephone.

20. Use discretion about the time and frequency of your calls to children.

21. Recognize that children will feel powerless and helpless and don't demean them, because they are so vulnerable.

22. Recognize that children may feel insecure and exhibit regressive behavior; be prepared to get them therapy if these behaviors persist.

23. Provide an appropriate role model for your children.

24. Allow your children to see where the other parent is going to live after moving out of the house.

25. Put your differences aside long enough to be able to peaceably attend school conferences and activities.

26. Recognize the rights and responsibilities of the other parent to consult school authorities concerning school performance and the right to inspect and receive copies of student records and reports and school calendars and notices.

27. Notify the other parent of medical emergencies, and recognize his or her right to have input about surgery, dental care, hospitalization, or institutionalization.

28. Recognize the right of both parents to inspect and receive copies of children's medical and dental records,

and the right to consult with any treating physician, dentist, or mental health professional.

29. Recognize that children need substantial contact with the same-gender parent during adolescence.

30. Allow all grandparents to continue having contact with the children whenever reasonable.

31. Communicate with the other parent openly, honestly, and regularly to avoid misunderstandings that could be harmful to your children.

32. Make plans directly with the other parent instead of using your children as go-betweens.

33. Live as close to one another as is practical, convenient, and reasonable.

34. Maintain household routines as much as possible to keep some stability in children's lives.

35. Maintain the same set of rules as much as possible in both homes.

Custody Don'ts

1. Don't agree to alternating, 50/50 placement arrangements.

2. Don't if possible, allow overnight visitation for infants (birth to 12 months).

3. Don't foster feelings of guilt in children over divorce.

4. Don't allow children 9 to 12 years of age to refuse to visit the other parent.

5. Don't allow teenagers to become too parental.

6. Don't allow children to exhibit too much acting out behavior in response to the divorce. If their behavior gets out of hand, don't deny them therapy.

7. Don't take sides about parenting issues in front of the children.

8. Don't put the children in the middle when arranging visitation.

9. Don't communicate with the other parent through the children.

10. Don't fight or argue with or degrade the other parent in front of the children.

11. Don't plan visitations with the children and then arrive late or not at all.

12. Don't withhold time with the other parent as punishment for the children and the other parent.

13. Don't discuss financial aspects of the divorce (support, maintenance, late or back payments) with the children.

14. Don't assume, based on your children's communication, anything about what the other parent has said or done. Check it out.

15. Don't use children as pawns to express anger toward the other parent.

16. Don't overburden children by requiring them to have too much responsibility for their growing up and maintenance.

17. Don't overburden children by giving them responsibility for maintaining your psychological stability.

18. Don't overburden children by making them the focus of arguments between you and the other parent.

19. Don't allow your children to spend too much time with a parent who appears to be or has been diagnosed as being mentally ill.

20. Don't separate your children.

21. Don't introduce children to every person you date.

22. Don't allow children to see sexually intimate behavior between you and your partner.

23. Don't sleep in the same bed with school-age children except under unusual circumstances.

24. Don't ask children to keep secrets from your ex-spouse.

Be mindful, at the outset of your divorce and throughout the entire process, of one of the primary rules—divorce adversely affects children and it is parents who determine the extent to which they are affected. The more of the dos you follow, the less adversely affected your children will be. The more of the don'ts you bring into your life, the more problems your children are likely to have. Many of the don'ts listed in this chapter were present in Chris's life.

If you are already steeped in divorce- and custody-related problems, it's probably not too late to change the way you are dealing with each other and your children. Few cases are ever really too late for implementing positive change. Children's minds are very malleable and if their parents start changing the way they handle situations, the children will start to change the way they react to them. This change is easier to bring about with very young and middle-school-age children than with teenagers, but they are children, nonetheless, and many of them will respond positively to appropriate changes.

We have now gone full circle in the hopes that you have recognized that WINNING CAN NEVER BE MORE IMPORTANT THAN THE WELL-BEING OF YOUR CHILDREN.

▼

Chapter

10

Resources Abound

Many types of mental health professionals can become involved in divorce cases and you may have difficulty differentiating one from another. This chapter will help you identify them, and will familiarize you with resources that can help you through the divorce process and its aftermath.

Selecting a therapist can be as difficult a process as selecting an attorney. Many different kinds of therapists are available, and you need to make sure that any therapist you go to is licensed or certified. Before going to the office of someone not licensed or certified, ask why. Being board certified and having a medical license is optimal for psychiatrists. Being licensed and listed in the National Register is most favorable for psychologists, and being licensed or certified is optimal for social workers or counselors.

Most state psychological associations have listings by area of psychologists specializing in divorce-related work. The National Register lists psychologists according to their areas of specialization. Also, ask your attorney for names of therapists with whom he or she has successfully worked. Word-of-mouth referrals for therapists are often the best reference because you know that someone has worked well and felt comfortable with a particular therapist.

The majority of marriage and family counseling is performed by social workers and counselors. When problems become more severe or involve significant concerns about developmental needs or deep-seated psychopathology, contacting a psychiatrist or psychologist is the way to go. If medication is needed for a severe psychiatric disorder, a psychiatrist would be the only individual to contact.

Psychiatrists

The Joint Commission on Interprofessional Affairs, which consists of representatives of the American Psychiatric Association, American Nurses' Association, American Psychological Association, and National Association of Social Workers, describes a psychiatrist as a physician whose specialty is diagnosis and treatment of people suffering from mental disorders. A properly-trained psychiatrist can provide a comprehensive psychiatric evaluation as well as a medical diagnosis, and then integrate a person's personal and medical history with the results of the examination and the tests to determine the best course of therapy and other treatments.

The United States has 37,000 practicing psychiatrists and psychiatric residents. After medical school, most go into a residency program for three years, where they continue their studies and provide supervised inpatient and outpatient clinical services.

Completion of the residency is not necessary for a physician to call himself or herself a psychiatrist. A small percentage request certification from the American Board of Psychiatry and Neurology, for which they must take oral and written exams after several years of practice, but about two-thirds of practicing psychiatrists are not board certified. A psychiatrist certified in psychiatry and neurology may take additional examinations to become certified in child psychiatry and/or forensic psychiatry. These examinations test basic competence, not expertise.

Psychologists

A psychologist is trained to study and measure mental processes and to diagnose and treat mental disorders. Use of this title is regulated by law in all 50 states. Psychologists are licensed to diagnose or treat behavioral, emotional, or mental disorders.

In most jurisdictions, a psychologist is someone who has a doctoral degree in psychology, either a Ph.D. or a Psy.D. The major difference between these two degrees is that the psychologist with a Ph.D. would have completed graduate training that included supervised experience in conducting research and would have conducted a research project as part of doctoral degree requirements. The Psy.D. may have no research experience. Someone with a Psy.D. degree would have completed a full-time predoctoral internship for a full year, usually involving both inpatient and outpatient treatment. If an attorney needs an expert with research experience, the Ph.D. is usually the better candidate. However, if the amount of predoctoral clinical experience is more important, the Psy.D. may have more than a Ph.D. with the same years of training.

There are five major areas of graduate study in psychology: clinical, counseling, school, industrial/organizational, and experimental. A subspecialty within clinical psychology is neuropsychology. In almost all states, psychologists are licensed generically, not as specialists, even though most psychologists are training as specialists in one of the areas mentioned. Licensing laws, state administrative codes, and professional ethical codes all require psychologists to practice solely within their area of training and competence. You must be careful to retain whichever type of psychologist has the training and demonstrated competence needed to testify as an expert in a particular area.

Finding a psychologist or other expert with the knowledge and experience you need for your case is difficult because as knowledge about areas of forensic practice grew, so did specialization in relatively narrow areas. Many psychologists and psychiatrists who offer general child and family services will not be up-to-the-minute on research and information in forensic child and family services. In a child custody case, you need a forensic expert.

Most of the experts an attorney may want to consult will be clinical psychologists, who are trained to evaluate and treat patients with severe psychological problems. Most Ph.D.s and virtually all Psy.D.s are clinical psychologists, and nearly all are licensed or eligible for licensure for independent practice.

People often ask what the difference is between psychiatry and clinical psychology. About 80 to 90 percent of what they do overlaps. However, the major distinction is that psychiatrists can prescribe medication and psychologists can administer, score, and interpret psychological tests. Psychiatrists have moved more toward the biological or organic aspects of mental health care and their expertise in prescribing medications has become a more central part of their work.

In the past, psychologists generally were not allowed to admit people to psychiatric hospitals. Patients were usually referred to psychiatrists who could hospitalize them. Today, depending on the state, psychologists are increasingly being allowed to admit patients to hospitals in conjunction with a psychiatrist or on their own.

Not all psychologists are trained to administer all psychological tests. This is especially true with regard to neuropsychological tests, which examine the central nervous system. Most psychologists can administer a screening test for brain damage, but few are skilled in the kind of neuropsychological testing that can establish, for example, which part of the brain is involved and how serious the deficit is. If these details are important to your case, your attorney should question the psychologist about his or her areas of expertise. It is best to have a board-certified neuropsychologist to do this kind of testing.

Counseling psychologists are trained to work with less severely mentally ill people. Most counseling psychologists are inadequately trained to administer or interpret projective tests, but they generally perform well when dealing with ongoing problems with day-to-day living. School psychologists are trained to evaluate, treat, and consult on educational problems of children and adolescents. They are trained in evaluating and dealing with learning problems. Industrial/organizational psychologists are trained to apply principles of psychology to business settings. Experimental psychologists are primarily teachers and researchers.

As I said before, most licensing of psychologists is generic, but some psychologists meet requirements set by some states for listing in the National Register of Health Service Providers in Psychology. Those requirements are:

- Currently licensed, certified, or registered by the state/provincial board of examiners of psychology at the independent practice level of psychology;
- A doctoral degree in psychology from a regionally accredited educational institution;
- Two years of supervised experience in health services in psychology, of which one year is in an organized health service training program and one year is at the postdoctoral level.

More than 16,000 psychologists are listed by the National Register. Whenever clinical or health expertise is relevant, an attorney would do well to retain a psychologist listed in this registry.

Social Workers

Social workers may have either a bachelor's or master's degree in social work and are trained to help people in the context of social and economic affairs. For example, a social worker may find a home that meets a person's special social, psychological, and physical needs. Many social workers are also able to evaluate children's developmental needs, parental emotional and economic stability, and each parent's ability to fulfill a child's emotional, social, and economic needs.

All 50 states, the District of Columbia, Puerto Rico, and the Virgin Islands license or certify social workers with master's degrees. Some states also license or certify those with bachelor's degrees. Because many people who have no educational background in the field are hired to do social work, it is necessary to ask about a social worker's training.

Social workers may receive certification through the Academy of Certified Social Workers (ACSW), within the National Association of Social Workers (NASW), and may use ACSW after their names once they are certified. Certification requires:

- Graduation from a school of social work accredited by the Council on Social Work Education;
- Two years of full-time paid social work practice beyond a graduate social work degree, or an equivalent amount of part-time professional practice;
- Regular NASW membership;
- Submission of three professional references;
- Successful completion of the ACSW examination.

Social workers who meet the requirements for ACSW certification can be listed in the NASW Register of Clinical Social Workers.

Social workers are not used as expert witnesses as often as psychologists and psychiatrists, but their expertise is sought in some cases. Social workers, for example, have testified in a number of appellate court cases involving child sexual abuse.

Professional Organizations

An essential part of an expert's qualifications is the list of organizations to which he or she belongs, particularly if membership is based in part or whole on a formal peer review rather than simply on payment of dues. "Fellow" status in professional organizations is predicated on such a review.

Psychiatrists

American Psychiatric Association represents about 70 percent of psychiatrists in the United States. Members must be physicians with some training and experience in psychiatry and pay annual dues. Fellows must have been members for at least eight years and have made significant contributions to psychiatry and to the association.

American Board of Psychiatry and Neurology grants certification in psychiatry, neurology, and child psychiatry based on examination.

American Psychoanalytic Association's members are psychoanalysts as well as psychiatrists.

American Board of Forensic Psychiatry grants certification in forensic psychiatry based on examinations.

American Academy of Psychiatry and Law is an organization of psychiatrists interested in the practice of and training in legal psychiatry. It does not certify. Any member of the American Psychiatric Association who is willing to pay the membership fee may join.

Psychologists

American Psychological Association limits full membership to psychologists with doctoral degrees (or master's degree associates for five years) who pay membership fees. Specialty areas are represented by separate divisions. Fellow status is granted to those who have made "unusual and outstanding contributions or performance in the field of psychology."

American Board of Professional Psychology confers diplomate status on psychologists in the areas of clinical, counseling, school, industrial/organizational, and neuropsychology based on examinations.

American Board of Forensic Psychology provides certification of psychologists in forensic psychology based on examinations. The American Board of Forensic Psychology and American Board of Professional Psychology have coordinated efforts in the area of forensic certification.

American Psychology–Law Society is a division of the American Psychological Association. Membership is open to those who pay the membership fee.

Social Workers

National Association of Social Workers is the primary membership organization for social workers. Membership is open to "professional social workers" who pay the dues.

Academy of Certified Social Workers is an administrative unit of the NASW Academy of Certified Social Workers and certifies master's degreed social workers who meet the criteria listed earlier.

National Organization of Forensic Social Work certifies as diplomates social workers who are heavily involved in providing social work consultation in the legal process. Certification is based on a review of training and experience, written work samples, and oral examination. All applicants must have at least a master's degree in social work and three years of post-master's experience.

Other Organizations

American Board of Medical Psychotherapists certifies psychologists, psychiatrists, social workers, and others with substantial knowledge and experience as medical psychotherapists.

American Orthopsychiatric Association is an interdisciplinary association for psychologists, psychiatrists, and social workers. Fellow status is offered to members in good standing for at least five years.

American Academy of Forensic Sciences promotes education and research in forensic sciences. Its members are organized into sections, with most mental health experts in the section of psychiatry and behavior science.

Handy Resources

The Good Divorce: Keeping Your Family Together When Your Marriage Comes Apart by Constance Ahrons, Harper, 1994.

The Divorce Source Book: Everything You Need to Know by Dawn Bradley Berry, J.D., Contemporary Books, 1992.

The Fresh Start Recovery Workbook by Robert Burns and Thomas Whiteman, Thomas Nelson Publishers, 1992.

The Five-Minute Lawyers Guide to Divorce by Michael and Ellen Cane, Dell Publishing, 1995.

Divorce and New Beginnings by Genevieve Clapp, John Wiley & Sons, 1992.

The Divorce Book for Men and Women by Harriet Newman Cohen and Ralph Gardner Jr., Avon Books, 1994.

Divorce Lawyers by Emily Couric, St. Martin's Press, 1992.

Divorce Help Source Book by Margorie Engel, Visible Inc. Press, 1994.

Vicki Lansky's Divorce Book for Parents by Vicki Lansky, Signet, 1988.

The Newly Divorced Book Protocol: How to Be Civil When You Hate Their Guts by Gloria Lintermans, Baracade Books, 1995.

Understanding Child Custody by Susan Newburg Turkel, Franklin Watts Press, 1991.

Crazy Time: Surviving Divorce by Abigail Trafford, Bantam Books, 1982.

Second Chances: Men, Women, and Children, a Decade After Divorce, Who Wins, Who Loses and Why by Judith Wallerstein and Sandra Blakesless, Houghton Mifflin, 1990.

Life After Divorce: Create a New Beginning by Karen Wegscheider-Cruse, Health Communications Press, 1994.

Children of Divorce by Sharlene Wolchik and Paul Karoly, Gardner Press, 1988.

Index